SATURDAY

T ST · MAYFAIR · LONDON

Vivienne
Westwood

LONDON

VIVIENNE WESTWOOD & JEWELLERY

FOREWORD
Andreas Kronthaler

INTRODUCTION
Alexander Fury

SPECIAL PHOTOGRAPHY
Philippe Lacombe

WITH 163 ILLUSTRATIONS

T&H

London, February 2025

To all Jewellery Lovers,

Jewellery helps you to be seen. Nothing does more to frame the face and give expression to the body and accentuate your personality.

Jewellery is powerful, and it can be loaded with meaning. It marks life, and it gives importance to it. Jewellery talks and, most importantly, it seduces the world around you.

From the very beginning, when I met Vivienne, we were interested in art and going to museums to study what people wore in the past.

We especially looked at the eighteenth century, when everybody wore pearls. Pearls became a Westwood classic. We wanted to make women look like they had just stepped out of the canvas. A moving picture that comes to life, in order to seduce the mind through the eyes.

My favourites, of course, are earrings. Vivienne loved earrings – she was never without, and changed them according to what she was wearing.

I love when earrings move; they constantly shout 'look at me!'

Jewellery is important for a designer. It's part of the appearance, just like hair or make-up. At Westwood, over time we built up a real treasure trove.

Even during the punk years, Vivienne incorporated studs, safety-pins, pin-up pictures, tins and bits of rubbish, bones, all kinds of things, appliquéd to clothes.

The orb logo itself is a jewel, symbolising the world with its past, its present and, through adding the Saturn ring, its future. It's very British and very Vivienne.

Early on in knowing each other, I saw this little Ancient Greek penis at an antique dealer's in the West End, which I mentioned to Vivienne, and the next day she gave it to me as a present; it became another Westwood lucky charm.

I care about craftsmanship and how things are made, and it's lovely to be able to share that through this book.

Love, Andreas

INTRODUCTION

ALEXANDER FURY

Safety-pins piercing faces. Pearl chokers and droplet earrings borrowed from Elizabethan portraits. Bondage chains and sado-masochistic buckled cuffs and dog-collars. Crowns and medallions and bejewelled regal orbs. The jewellery vocabulary of Vivienne Westwood is as distinct and immediately recognisable as that of her clothing, her corsets and mini-crinolines, her tartans and bondage trousers. It is a distinct look, one both integrated into her fashion and standing apart; an expression of her unique aesthetic sensibility but, more importantly, of her ideology and deep-seated belief systems. Westwood's jewellery both embraced culture and exploded it; trotted the globe, while remaining distinctly, even parochially, British. In her hands, that aforementioned safety-pin might adorn the face of a queen, while her prim pearls could be worn by punks.

Jewellery by its nature is a detail, adornment, the finishing touch. One can be clothed without jewellery, yet jewellery adds to the notion of being 'dressed', or perhaps more accurately, dressed up. It is the unnecessary gilding on the lily, the cherry on top of the cake. Yet jewellery has existed before fashion, rough-hewn jewels and totems dating back to prehistoric times – a means of asserting status, or indicating affiliation to groups, friends or foes. In Ancient Greece and Rome, while citizens were clad in draped cloth (the simple belted and pinned geometric forms of the peplos, chiton or toga), jewellery was already elaborate and highly finished, inlaid with precious gems and enamel.

Jewellery was certainly no afterthought to Westwood, who appreciated those historical antecedents, chiming with her own fascination with the past. For the Westwood fashion shows of the 1990s, devised by Westwood and her husband Andreas Kronthaler in rich creative partnership, intricate sketches detailed every aspect of each 'total look', including painstakingly illustrated accessories and intricate bijoux.[1] Indeed, jewellery was, for Westwood, one of the first means to express her creative urges, her impulse to design. She was born Vivienne Isabel Swire, near the town of Glossop, in Derbyshire, on 8 April 1941. Both of her parents worked with their hands: her father came from a family of shoe-makers, while her mother worked in the Cheshire cotton mills, and was an adept knitter – a skill she passed on to her daughter. Born into wartime frugality and rationing, the young Westwood was a craftswoman: as a teenager, she sewed her own clothes, and later declared, 'Honestly, at the age of five, I could have made a pair of shoes.'[2] A love of making was at the root of Westwood's creative practice from its earliest expression.

And that expression first came to the public through jewellery. One of the earliest lessons Westwood learned in fashion was through jewellery: 'I was always interested in extremes,' Westwood wrote in her memoir, recalling a moment at a dance when she was 15. 'There was this fashion for large plastic daisy earrings, but I made enormous earrings out of giant marguerites. I remember the band leader stopped the music when I came in and said, "Look, everyone, at that amazing girl, in those earrings."'[3] Westwood's designs always sought to attract attention – and even on the quietest outfit, her jewellery was always a talking-point.

Aged 17, Westwood moved with her family from the rural north to the London suburb of Harrow, to run a post office. Westwood enrolled in Harrow Art School, where she first studied fashion. 'I didn't like it, we had to draw all the time, and I wanted to make clothes,' she recalled.[4] So she transferred to silversmithing – an art in which she could work with her hands to effect change. Although she left the school after one term, for the rest of her life this remained her only formal training in design. A deep thinker and intellectual with a passion for learning, Westwood nevertheless constantly expressed herself through making: this focus on jewellery was an early manifestation of that. This education was also a point of connection between her own heritage and that of Andreas Kronthaler, who studied goldsmithing as a teenager in the Austrian city of Graz, six hours from his own birthplace in the rural Ziller Valley of the Tyrol. Both would be fascinated by jewellery throughout their three-decade-long collaboration.

With typical pragmatism, however, the teenaged Westwood reasoned she could not make a living from creative endeavours and instead, in 1959, began to train to become a teacher at Saint Gabriel's College in Camberwell. Three years later, she married Derek Westwood – and made her own wedding dress. Jewellery only came back to the Westwood story after her divorce: first, when selling her designs on a stall in London's Portobello Market as her only source of income in the mid-1960s, and again, five years later, when she began to work with the music impresario Malcolm McLaren, laying the foundations for the movement later known as punk in their boutique at 430 King's Road, which opened in 1971. McLaren and Westwood first bonded, in part, over Westwood's mother's kitchen table, where Westwood created her jewellery pieces alongside conversation with McLaren. And the impetus to open their own store came, in part, from Westwood's own experience as a saleswoman – her teenage background in her parents' post office, but also selling her own designs on the Portobello Road.

On the King's Road, Westwood was once again making: for the first incarnation of her and McLaren's boutique, dedicated to Fifties retro and Teddy Boy style and named 'Let It Rock' (1971–72), Westwood painstakingly unpicked the 'Drape' suits of the latter subcultural movement to copy in flashy Lurex and fake fur, learning by doing. While jewellery didn't feature per se, Westwood did create exceptional hybrid pieces, crossing jewellery with clothing. T-shirts were pock-marked with studs, draped with chains or scarred with zips, the pulls positioned across the chest to resemble nipple-rings; even more extreme, a series of T-shirts, struck with thick metal chains, were adorned with chicken bones spelling out epithets: 'Rock', 'Perv', 'Scum', 'Fuck'. Sourced from Westwood and McLaren's dinner plates, the meat was boiled from the bones, which were then painstakingly drilled and connected with chain links, and attached to the T-shirts with metal studs. Assembled by Westwood herself at her own kitchen table, they were laborious and time-consuming works, each taking approximately a day to create.

Interestingly, bones would emerge again and again in Westwood's jewellery, connecting her designs back to the most stereotypically simple totemic adornments of prehistoric man. In 1995, designing a collection titled 'Vive la Cocotte', Westwood and Andreas Kronthaler created earrings of dangling miniature skeletons. The idea,

Kronthaler said, connected with the notion of the cocotte as a courtesan, but re-cast her as 'man-eater', wearing the entrails of her prey.[5] The jointed figure also connects with the idea of man as puppet, a link with the 1898 novel *La Femme et le pantin* by Pierre Louÿs, adapted by director Josef von Sternberg to a 1935 film starring Marlene Dietrich. Literature always inspired Westwood – and Louÿs, an author whose work aimed to 'express pagan sensuality with stylistic perfec-tion',[6] tied perfectly with her interests. And that Dietrich movie was one of the direct inspirations behind Westwood's Autumn – Winter 1992/93 collection, and it was Andreas Kronthaler's favourite film. Later, Westwood and Kronthaler devised jewellery literally shaped as bones, their familiar forms set with pavé crystals and combined with classic historical motifs such as ribbon bows and teardrops, fusing the dainty with the bloodthirsty, the nihilistic nuances of punk rock with the kind of jewellery worn by painter Thomas Gainsborough's heroines. Bones also had plenty of antecedents in jewellery – traditionally featured in memento mori and mourning jewellery, or presented like religious reliquaries.

The 'Let It Rock' jewellery-clothing pieces are extraordinary; in hindsight, they give indications as to many directions Westwood would pursue in both her fashion and jewellery designs. Of course, they are among the earliest incarnations of the slogan T-shirts which would become one of the mostly widely recognised elements of the punk style concocted by Westwood and McLaren; and they connect with primitive themes of prehistoric adornment that Westwood would be fascinated with through-out her career, as well as the ideas of bricolage, a French term roughly translated as 'Do It Yourself', more commonly applied to art created from unconventional and non-traditional materials. The same was true of Westwood's clothes – encouraged by McLaren, whose art school background brought ideas such as bricolage and *objets trouvés* ('found objects') to her practice.

But there is even a connection with a deeper, grander past, with Renaissance clothes weighted with precious jewels: the pearl-encrusted costumes of Queen Elizabeth I, for example, were arguably more jewellery than garment. Westwood referenced those later, creating tweed jackets with crystals pushing through slashes in the cloth (Autumn – Winter 1991/92), as well as evening dresses and men's jackets crusted with pearl embroideries (Autumn – Winter 1995/96). It's a stretch, but you could connect those, too, with 430 King's Road's second incarnation, inspired by black-leather-clad rockers and re-named 'Too Fast To Live, Too Young To Die' (1972–74). Westwood would stud leather jackets with metal and festoon them with yet more chains. And as early as the late 1970s, Westwood had begun to speak about the connections between history and her clothes, declaring in a rare television interview in 1978 that a kilt designed for the store – renamed 'Seditionaries' in 1976 – was reminiscent of 'Greek peasant costume'.[7] 'It's got an old sort of feeling,' Westwood stated of her designs. 'Something that you might have seen at the Battle of Culloden.'[8]

As punk developed, its look became more complex – and true jewellery began to figure. At SEX (1974–76), the King's Road boutique's third incarnation, buckled dog-collars and cuffs were sold as jewellery, purchased wholesale from early '70s British leather fetish purveyor The London Leatherman. At this point, many of Westwood and McLaren's wares were pre-existing pieces that were customised rather than wholly original – which continued in the shop's later incarnation as Seditionaries. 'I do remember someone coming in to sell razor-blade jewellery,' Westwood recalled in her memoir;[9] she did not originate the notion of razor-blade jewellery that would become a punk icon, but it was created in emulation of Westwood and McLaren's own distinctive style. Indeed, their wardrobe propositions were unlike anything else previously seen. While Westwood used high-quality wools and tartans for her bondage clothes, her approach to jewellery, in particular, bucked against all received norms.

The ultimate 'jewel' of punk wasn't the razor-blade (the edges blunted with a nail-file), but rather the humble, industrial safety-pin, taken as it was, decorating clothing and puncturing bodies, given the same prominence as precious bijoux. Indeed, by using it to pierce an image of Elizabeth II – as featured on the cover art of the Sex Pistols' 1977 single 'God Save the Queen', designed by Jamie Reid, and on one of Westwood and McLaren's Seditionaries T-shirts – she arguably transmogrified the humble pin into a 'crown jewel'. Appropriately enough, almost two decades later, in Westwood's 'Anglomania' show (Autumn – Winter 1993/94), the safety-pin would appear in a refined form, albeit still piercing the cheek of her tartan-clan 'queen' both in her show and on the invite (Elizabeth I this time). Regardless of Westwood's shifting sensibilities and loyalties throughout her career, she would return again and again to these punk impulses. Twenty years later, Westwood produced a collection throwing back to the glories of Elizabethan costume and titled 'Five Centuries Ago'. In the accompanying advertising campaign, photographed by Gian Paolo Barbieri, the model Jerry Hall appears as Gloriana herself, clutching scepter and orb, but along-side crouches Westwood's own son Ben as a 'punk favourite', dressed in a miniature crown – but also a leather dog-collar that could have come straight from SEX.

In retrospect these propositions, sometimes seemingly juvenile and nose-thumbing, with the spittle-flecked vitriol of teenage rebellion, served as serious and lasting challenges to traditional ideas of beauty and adornment. As with Westwood's best work, they embody her deep-seated anti-orthodox stance: she most frequently quoted the British twentieth-century philosopher Bertrand Russell, declaring that 'orthodoxy is the grave of intelligence'.[10] Her rejections of the standard and the accepted exerted seismic influence on the aesthetics of culture as a whole, while Westwood and McLaren's outright anarchy upended the fashion industry. Echoes of their styles and approaches can be seen across Westwood's work for the next 50 years – a consistent rebellion, and a questioning of the status quo. That is perhaps more expected in fashion, where past styles are constantly challenged, torn down, and contradicted by shifts in mode. But the value of jewellery has, by contrast, been held sacrosanct, even unyielding. Westwood's work exploded those notions, in a challenge as signifi-cant as Gabrielle Chanel's embracing of costume jewellery as a high fashion status symbol in the 1920s. If Chanel championed the fake, Westwood elevated the everyday, reasoning that anything – everything – could be precious. In her 1983 'Punkature' collection, Westwood punctured the tin lids of scouring-powder containers with holes to feature as jewel-like buttons, and bent disused kitchen spoons into jewellery. Over a quarter of a century later, in reflection of her belief in 'Do It Yourself' and recycling tied to ecological concerns, Westwood and Kronthaler would design intricate eighteenth-century-style necklaces and earrings crafted from discarded soft-drink cans, their workmanship as precious as any antique bijou.

As indicated by the ever-shifting aesthetics and obsessions of the shop at 430 King's Road, a restless motion between ideas and ideals was a characteristic of Westwood's work throughout her career. She would abandon the 'urban guerrilla' look of punk for the swashbuckling romance of seventeenth-century pirates, committing herself to presenting on the catwalk and therefore to a constant inbuilt obsolescence and seasonal renewal that characterises the fashion industry. In contrast to the destruction and chaos of punk, when designing under her own name in the mid-1980s, following the dissolution of her partnership with McLaren, Westwood decided to openly embrace history, art and culture. Her collections referenced the Renaissance and Baroque, and alluded to classical Greco-Roman themes and iconographies – an embrace of literature and art accompanied by a deep-seated belief in the power of culture and education to expand horizons, and in the worth of history, so often abandoned in a relentless pursuit of modernity. She saw her collections as a cultural crusade. Later, Westwood's sensibilities changed again, her long-lasting and deep-rooted belief in environmental and political activism coming to the fore in her designs, using her collections to convey her polemic.

Despite these ever-changing ideals – and accompanying switches in aesthetic obsessions – Westwood used her collections to define 'classics', a canon of items that served to represent her look and approach to dressing, not least through jewellery. It was during the late 1980s that the notion of 'Vivienne Westwood Jewellery' truly began to take shape, when the designer expanded her universe and started to define motifs, items and systems of dressing allied to her design philosophies. Notably, her clothes became about refinement, rooted in revolutionary revivals of hitherto archaic modes of dress, and in that idea of 'dressing up', against a prevalent cultural mood of dressing down in sportswear. Westwood even used that phrase as the title for her Autumn – Winter 1991/92 collection, which marked her own-label Paris debut, standing in direct contrast to the mood of her moment. But its roots were there back in 1987, when Westwood presented a collection named 'Harris Tweed', inspired by British tailoring and 'aristocratic' styles influenced by the royal family. From piercing the Queen's face with safety-pins, Westwood was now emulating her dress.

It was within this collection that the designer first introduced two icons of the Westwood jewellery canon, still with us today: her first pearls, and the first orb. Pearls were an obvious reference, in a collection inspired by the upper classes: Westwood presented them as single-string necklaces, worn with staid twinsets knitted from fine wool by the British manufacturer John Smedley. Westwood always liked to *épater les bourgeois* by twisting the known. In her jewellery, as in her clothes, often the simplest act was of appropriation or displacement: in 'Harris Tweed', her hyperclassic pearls worn by male models gave a similar sense of disquiet to her later codpieces for women, or the arresting 'Tits' T-shirt of 1977, printed with an image of bared female breasts, which Westwood always asserted was best worn by a man. One of the influences on Westwood's re-introduction of the classic look was, even then, a decade old: she recalled how Jordan – on paper, the shop assistant at SEX and Seditionaries, but in actual practice a punk icon due to her unique and arresting visual sense – wore a conservative twinset and pearls to unsettling effect at the very height of punk.

Westwood's pearls, therefore, also carried the spirit of punk with them. Later, she would expand on them, proposing pearls as part of her Autumn – Winter 1990/91 'Portrait' collection. 'I thought the idea of one pearl earring or … three strands of pearls with a pearl drop in the middle was typical of all jewellery,' Westwood stated. 'You could fit it with practically any period and it would look great. So I chose things in that way, I wanted them to be complete, and as archetypal as they could be.'[11]

Pearls, of course, are heavy with the kind of symbolism that always appealed to Westwood: she loved clothing that spoke, that expressed something deeper and more meaningful than their mere surface. Here, think of pearls of wisdom, as an idiom, and the history of pearls worn in great works of art, whose subject-matter inspired that 'Portrait' show. 'There's nothing more flattering than pearls,' says Andreas Kronthaler, who first worked with Westwood on the 'Portrait' collection and is today creative director of the brand. 'They play with the whites of your eyes and teeth; pearls really talk to you. And they work on everybody – from young to old, women and men, everyone.'[12]

The Westwood orb emblem, redolent of tradition yet with a 'Saturn ring' spanning its circumference, actually originated in Westwood's 'Mini Crini' collection (Spring – Summer 1986). It was, however, first used in jewellery for 'Harris Tweed', where the orb appeared as a pendant necklace. The orb itself is, of course, a royal symbol, inherently English, and was borrowed by Westwood from the Harris Tweed Authority, who used it as emblems on labels authenticating their product. When Westwood designed her first watch with the Swiss company Swatch in 1993, it came packaged in a jewel-like orb, which models carried down her catwalk like a relic of imperial regalia. As with Harris Tweed, it became a mark of quality and identity for Westwood, her own regalia, an emblem embedded in her pearl necklaces and earrings or set with crystals. Yet the story of the orb was deeper than its surface: Westwood embedded everything she designed with meaning and symbolism, narratives and intellectual weight. Spinning a Saturn ring around the orb was, for Westwood, more than an update of a pre-existing symbol: if the orb represents history and heritage, the Saturn ring symbolises innovation and progress, looking forwards while simultaneously glancing back, taking the past into the future. In essence, it epitomises Westwood's entire approach to fashion.

Of course, history is essential when examining Westwood's approach to jewellery. As with her clothes, she precisely examined and recreated styles from the past, often combining different approaches and eras to intriguing and even unsettling effect. This propensity was pushed further by her partnership with Andreas Kronthaler and his own interest in jewellery, and through their work with Laurent Rivaud, creative director of Vivienne Westwood jewellery since the mid-1990s. Colliding classical elements with ideas from Westwood's punk era, they upended and challenged classic forms and approaches – as Marcel Proust wrote, the remembrance of things past is not necessarily the remembrance of things as they were. Hence Westwood and Kronthaler twisted the past, inventing their own language of jewellery alongside their clothes. As in the 1970s, the two mediums continued to clash: in 'Harris Tweed', Westwood created crowns pieced together from the collection's namesake woolen fabric, whose colours she appreciated because, she stated, they were 'like jewels'.[13]

Later, for the Spring – Summer 1992 'Salon' collection, Westwood dressed the model Sara Stockbridge in a metal chastity belt under a billowing wedding dress of torn tulle. The belt was forged by Franz Kronthaler, Andreas's father, who was a blacksmith in the Tyrol.

As in her fashion, in jewellery Westwood would return to re-examine themes and influences, as if discovering them anew. The collections from the late 1980s onwards played with classical drapery, expected in fluid fabrics like silk jersey cut into brief toga dresses, yet unanticipated, even revolutionary, when fused with classical tailoring or corsets, or cut in crisp taffeta. Equally, Westwood toyed with classical themes in the jewellery: the influence of Ancient and often Pagan Greece, specifically, was essential. In 1987, Westwood designed a set of horns, in clear resin attached to a thick leather band and worn across the forehead by models in her Spring – Summer 1988 show, aptly titled 'Britain Must Go Pagan'. In 2004, for the 'Exhibition' collection – inspired in part by the Vivienne Westwood retrospective at the Victoria and Albert Museum in London – this design was reworked, newly refined in brass with pavé crystal. Referencing the satyr, a lustful, drunken woodland god of Greek mythology, these pieces connected with Westwood's celebration of human sexuality – and an innate connection of the wearing of jewellery with attraction or seduction. Westwood sported her horn design herself, and Andreas Kronthaler says that these horns are his favourite piece of Vivienne Westwood jewellery. Indeed, jewellery was a point of connection between Westwood and Kronthaler: they exchanged gifts to demonstrate their love, and these often in turn served to inspire creations in their own collections.

In 1989, for her 'Pagan V' collection, the last in a series explicitly exploring themes drawn from Greco-Roman civilisation, Westwood emblazoned the word 'SEX' across a chain choker, inspired by a visit to an exhibition of Ancient Greek jewellery at the British Museum. It seems unusual source-material for such a statement, but Westwood was fascinated with the sexual mores proudly evident in ancient cultures: one of her first gifts to Andreas Kronthaler was a phallus pendant, an original Ancient Greek artefact – obviously emblematic of virility – purchased on Conduit Street, near her flagship store. That phallus would be reproduced and used in Westwood jewellery – and the motif had earlier been used as buttons in her 'Hypnos' collection, which also explored Greek pagan imagery. Greece returned again and again: close study of the publication *Greek Gold: Jewellery of the Classical World*, a catalogue that accompanied a 1994 exhibition at New York's Metropolitan Museum of Art, surrendered multiple ancient motifs that would inspire Westwood jewels. The permanence of jewellery, passed between different generations as heirlooms, appealed to Westwood, playing into her deep belief that history had meaning, that the past was of value.

Equally expressive of that love of Ancient Greece and Rome, myth and fable often inspired Westwood. She was a quintessentially British designer, in that her clothes were a form of storytelling, couched in a richly imagined narrative, its twists and turns justifying creative endeavours. In that respect, she connected with allegorical and narrative painters of the Regency period, and pulled characters from their canvases, such as the Italian Commedia dell'Arte theatrical figures featured in the eighteenth-century paintings of Antoine Watteau. There are also references to traditional British legends, as well as Mitteleuropa fairy-tales, echoing Kronthaler's childhood: both illustrate Westwood's life-long enthusiasm for literature. She once stated that the best accessory is a book. Her jewellery often explores notions of the fantastical, the unreal and fairy-tale. Scale is exaggerated, colours are shifted, elements are unexpected, like different worlds thrown together. Snails are cast in silver as brooches that 'slither' across bodies, as if plucked from the bucolic pastoral idylls of one of Westwood's favourite artists, François Boucher. On the flip-side, a thick chain necklace named 'Guinevere', in homage to the medieval British legend of King Arthur, resembles a relic pulled directly from the past in heavy oxidised brass.

Pirates were the inspiration for Westwood's first-ever catwalk show, and that notion of exploration – and of plunder – has run throughout her work. She referenced other cultures as she referred to other times, examining differing belief systems, aesthetics and methodologies of craft to discover new ways of creating. Today, the Vivienne Westwood brand actively collaborates with the Ethical Fashion Initiative of the International Trade Centre to work with artisans in Kenya, Nepal, Burkina Faso and Mali to celebrate indigenous craft. Her exploration always had authenticity, respect and truth at its core. Connected with Westwood's innate unorthodoxy, her celebration of global identity is an act of cultural appreciation and a challenge to Western cultural imperialism. As such, Westwood's 'talismans' include items like dangling Eiffel Towers and Austrian cowbells, alongside apparent souvenirs from far-flung locales, imbued with the identity of their place of creation.

Détournement is the Situationist principle of appropriating existing work, then 'remixing' it, subverting its meaning to create antagonism and uproar. You don't hear it used in a fashion context – maybe because it sounds pretentious. And maybe because fashion generally does the opposite, filching from the counter-culture to sanitise, anaesthetise and sell to the masses. Yet it is at the root of all Westwood has created, especially how she both celebrated and denigrated history to challenge and provoke. Westwood's obsession with the eighteenth century, which she considered a high point of art and culture, saw its characteristic jewellery both celebrated and twisted. The idea of the parure, a co-ordinating suite of several jewellery pieces, highly finished and designed to be worn together, was explored often, as were other traditional antique jewellery pieces, often executed in unconventional materials – recycled detritus composing elaborate girandole earrings; papier mâché as a diadem – or with traditional elements like teardrop gems and ribbon bows contrasted with Westwood's lexicon of motifs which included phalluses, vulvas and miniature corsets. In other pieces, she even seemed to prise the finishings of eighteenth-century cabinets and chairs from their pieces to slap them into her jewellery: a charm necklace might dangle prancing satyrs or the empty ornate gilt frame of a Baroque masterpiece.

Trash transmogrified to treasure, history revitalised, a dusty orb spun with a Saturn ring atop to become a symbol of forward-thinking and ceaseless innovation. Vivienne Westwood's jewellery designs are as rich and symbol-laden as any of her fashion inventions. Each bears witness to Westwood's constant questioning of value systems – decorative, fiscal, sexual – and her stalwart refusal, ever, to conform.

THE RAREST
THINGS IN
THE WORLD,
NEXT TO A SPIRIT
OF DISCERNMENT,
ARE DIAMONDS
AND PEARLS.

JEAN DE LA BRUYÈRE[14]

Anglomania Necklace

Andreas Kronthaler for Vivienne Westwood 'Tintwistle' AW 23/24

ORIGINS

Vivienne Westwood's abiding signature, from her earliest creative endeavours, was a rejection of the orthodox. She seized upon unexpected ideas to produce work that was wildly original. In the evolution of her unique aesthetic language, jewellery was a fundamental component – part of a 'total look' that expressed her ever-shifting ideal of beauty. Throughout Westwood's career, she returned to specific obsessions that had shaped her since childhood. We can see the origins of her style in both early examples of her work and emblematic pieces that typify the Westwood look. Sex is omnipresent, referencing the libertine mores of ancient cultures, 1950s pin-ups, and the padlocks and buckled cuffs of BDSM subcultures. Her activism is also writ large – literally, in terms of political slogans, but also more fundamentally in her use of recycled forms and materials, demonstrating her deep commitment to ecological concerns. Skulls and crossbones reappear – emblematic of pirates, nodding to her first catwalk show in 1981, as well as the motif of her shop in its 'Too Fast To Live, Too Young To Die' incarnation. Punk and politics, safety-pins and badges, chaos and chains: these are vibrant hallmarks that communicate Westwood's philosophy, and they sit at the heart of the house today.

Pin Badges
'Climate Revolution' SS 13

Christa Brooch
'Europa' SS 17

Kate Safety Pin, modelled by Kate Moss,
'Anglomania' AW 93/94

Kate Safety Pin
'Anglomania' AW 93/94

S&M Earrings
Andreas Kronthaler for Vivienne Westwood 'OK... It's Showtime' SS 19

Shackle Earrings
Andreas Kronthaler for Vivienne Westwood 'Vivienne' AW 18/19

Malia Earrings
Andreas Kronthaler for Vivienne Westwood 'Mayfair Lady' AW 21/22

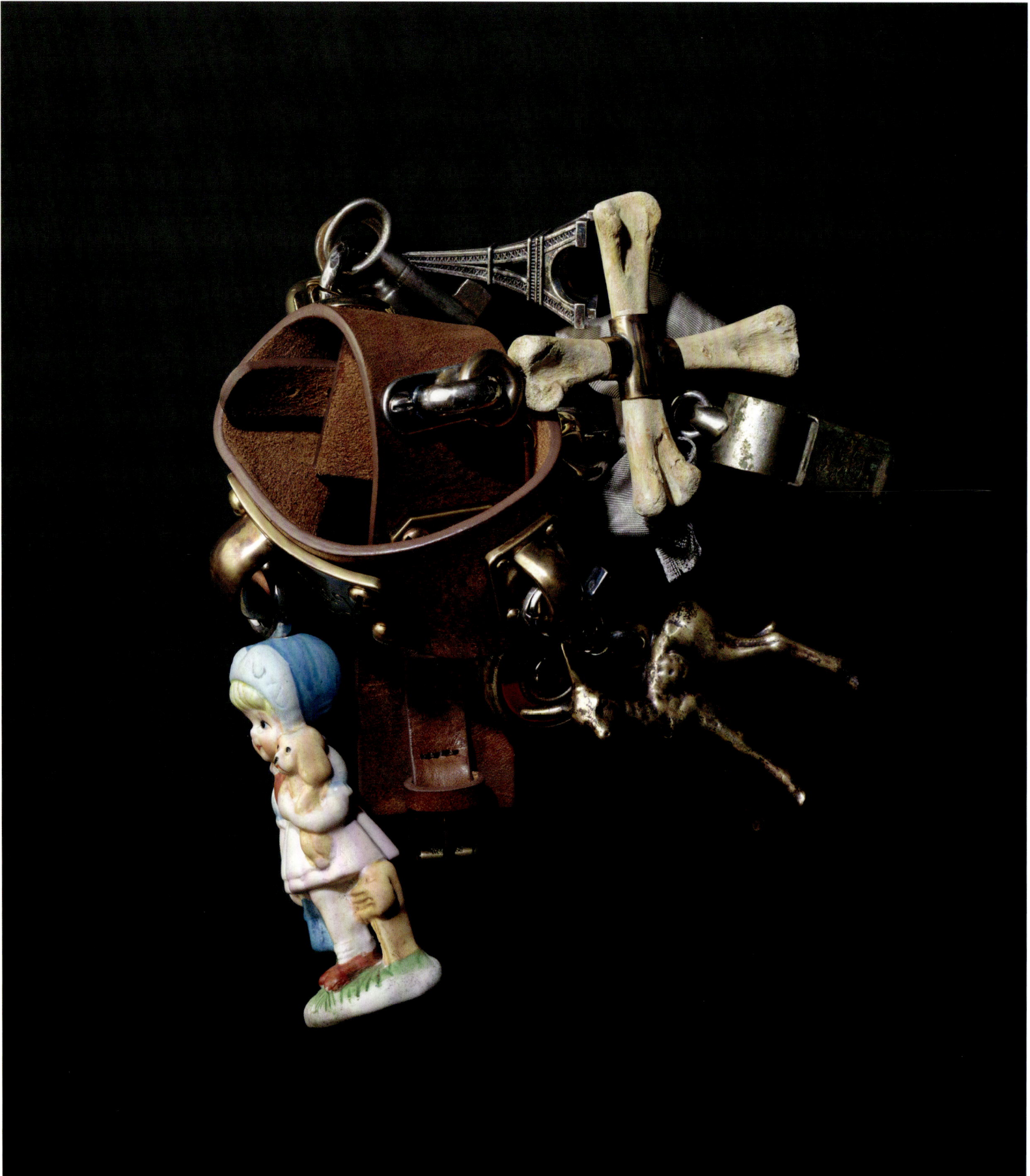

Gillian Choker

Andreas Kronthaler for Vivienne Westwood 'The Tailor' AW 24/25

Super Elevated Ghillie Shoes
'Anglomania' AW 93/94

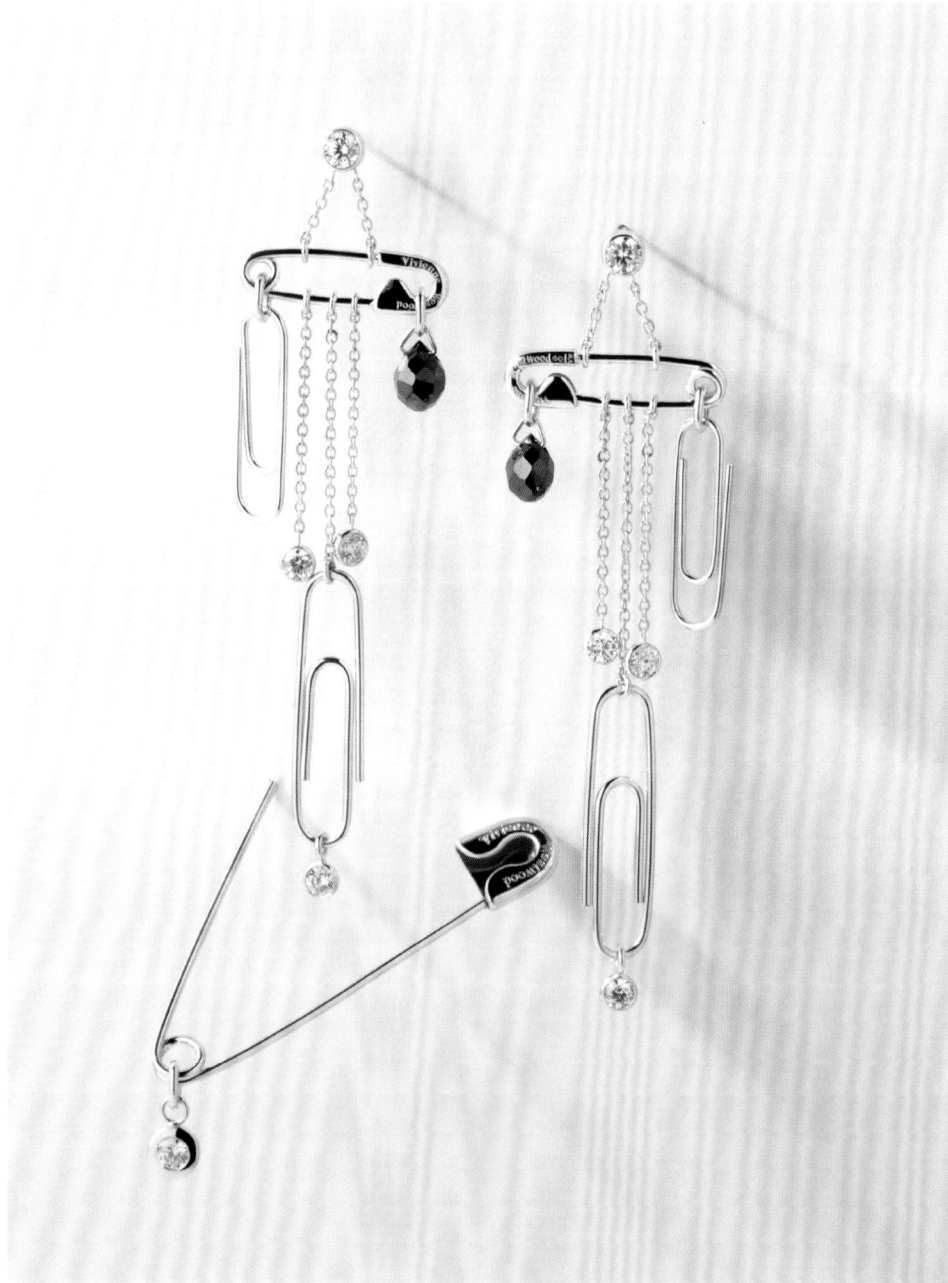

Hardcore Earrings
'Propaganda' AW 05/06

Roman Necklace
UNISEX SS 19

Sigrid Choker
Andreas Kronthaler for Vivienne Westwood 'Tintwistle' AW 23/24

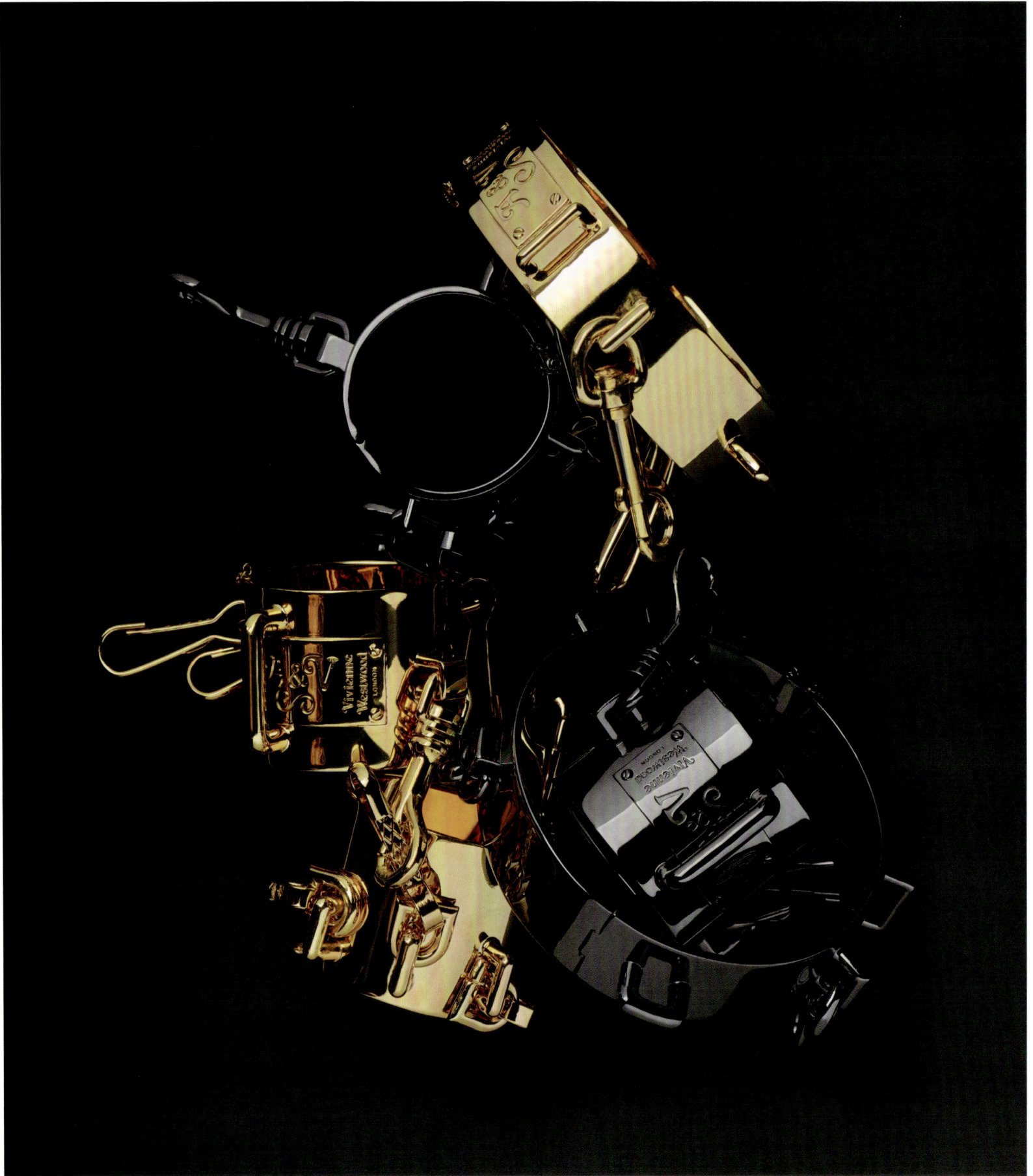

S&M Cuffs

Andreas Kronthaler for Vivienne Westwood 'OK... It's Showtime' SS 19

S&M Chokers

Andreas Kronthaler for Vivienne Westwood 'OK... It's Showtime' SS 19

Cordelia Chokers

Andreas Kronthaler for Vivienne Westwood 'La Nouvelle Eve' AW 22/23

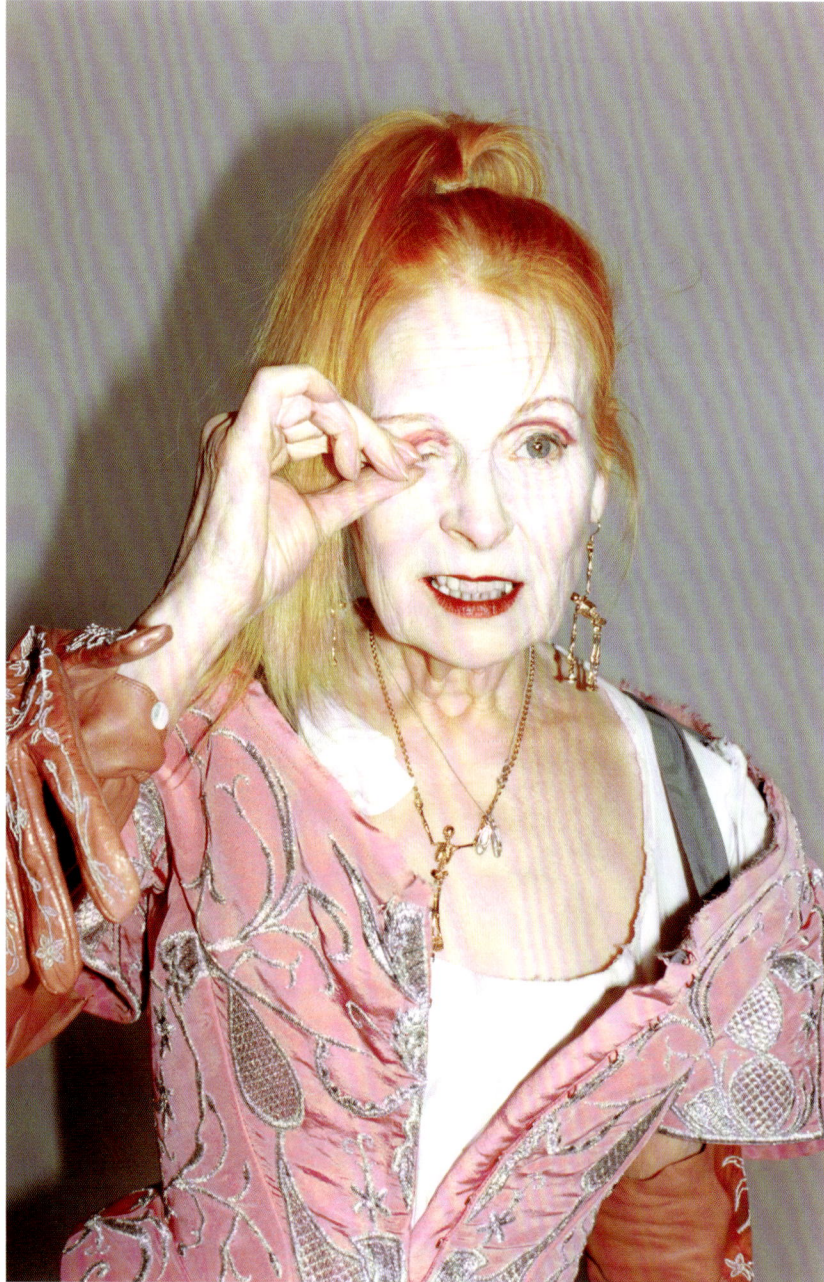

Skeleton Necklace and Earring
'On Liberty' AW 94/95

I Am Not a Terrorist Choker
'Ultra Femininity' SS 05

Chaos Necklace
'World Wide Woman' AW 11/12

Giant Skeleton Necklace
'Climate Revolution' SS 13

Detail of S&M Cuffs & Choker (see p. 38)
Andreas Kronthaler for Vivienne Westwood 'OK... It's Showtime' SS 19

Curtain Hook Earrings
Andreas Kronthaler for Vivienne Westwood 'OK... It's Showtime' SS 19

Broken Pearl Necklace
'Storm in a Teacup' AW 96/97

PEARLS

In her 'Portrait' collection for Autumn – Winter 1990/91, Vivienne Westwood debuted the now-iconic Three Row Pearl Drop Choker. Among her sources of inspiration were the romantic French paintings, ceramics and furnishings assembled by the 4th Marquess of Hertford in the nineteenth century, housed at the Wallace Collection in London. Taking pearls from their conventional aristocratic context, Westwood gave them a new and desirable edge. As she once stated, 'Art should never be sociological; it has got to be timeless. It's got to be your vision and how you can represent the world you see.'[15] In typical Westwood fashion, her pieces were unisex: male as well as female models paraded on the catwalk, adorned with pearls. Still, Westwood insisted on upholding the highest standards of craftsmanship: each necklace is hand-strung, and every pearl is individually hand-knotted. Evolving the look in line with sustainable farming practices, the house today uses glass pearls, as well as freshwater pearls. Statement pieces and timeless classics, these sensual masterworks – whether in natural ivory or muted pastels – have become a signature of the house.

Athena Necklace
'Erotic Zones' SS 95

Azaela Earrings
Andreas Kronthaler for Vivienne Westwood 'Andreas' SS 18

Gypsy Pearl Choker
'Erotic Zones' SS 95

Three Row Pearl Drop Necklace
'Portrait' AW 90/91

Three Row Bas Relief Choker
'Salon' SS 92

Gabriella Neck Rings
Andreas Kronthaler for Vivienne Westwood '43. Old Town' SS 24

Bagatelle Pearl Choker
'Vive la Bagatelle' SS 97

Sidonie Earrings
'I am Expensiv' SS 07

Gladys Earrings
Andreas Kronthaler for Vivienne Westwood '43. Old Town' SS 24

Loulia Earrings
Andreas Kronthaler for Vivienne Westwood '12' SS 22

Rosario Earring
Andreas Kronthaler for Vivienne Westwood 'Vivienne' AW 18/19

Gina Earring
Andreas Kronthaler for Vivienne Westwood '12' SS 22

Athena Necklace (see p. 46), modelled by Kate Moss,
'Erotic Zones' SS 95

Fulco Necklace
Andreas Kronthaler for Vivienne Westwood '7' AW 19/20

Venus Pearl Earrings
Andreas Kronthaler for Vivienne Westwood 'Calibrate' SS 25

Loulia Necklace
Andreas Kronthaler for Vivienne Westwood '12' SS 22

Nymph Earrings
'Nymphs' SS 02

Papier Mâché Tiara
'Winter' AW 00/01

DROPS & BOWS

Vivienne Westwood was passionate about the eighteenth century, which she considered a high point of culture. Her work from the late 1980s onwards contained multiple allusions to the art, literature and philosophy of the Age of Enlightenment. Her use of the parure (since the time of the court of Louis XIV, the term has denoted a suite of highly finished jewellery pieces, designed to be worn together) is a direct reflection of her love of the era, with its distinctive decorative forms, such as droplets, bows, hearts and flowers. But Westwood toyed with the language of these archetypal tropes. Scale is often overblown, challenging our preconceptions of archival jewellery by giving delicate pieces new impact through a bold reconsideration of proportion. Alongside painstakingly worked precious metals, Westwood also proposed unusual and rustic materials, colours and shapes. With her refusal to conform and constant questioning of value systems, crystal and silver could easily be replaced with papier mâché or recycled cans. These designs – never static; always devised in dynamic rapport with the body – frame the face, underscore conversation, and attract attention to the intelligence and life force of the wearer.

Papier Mâché Tiara and Earrings
'Winter' AW 00/01

Papier Mâché Earrings
'Winter' AW 00/01

Josie Necklace
Andreas Kronthaler for Vivienne Westwood 'Mayfair Lady' AW 21/22

Gainsborough Necklace
'Climate Revolution' SS 13

Gainsborough Coronet
'Climate Revolution' SS 13

Justina Earrings, modelled by Andreas Kronthaler,
Andreas Kronthaler for Vivienne Westwood 'Down to No. 10' SS 21

Georgian Necklace
AW 13/14 Collection

Isaura Necklace
Andreas Kronthaler for Vivienne Westwood 'Tintwistle' AW 23/24

Isaura Tiara
Andreas Kronthaler for Vivienne Westwood 'Tintwistle' AW 23/24

Isaura Earrings
Andreas Kronthaler for Vivienne Westwood 'Tintwistle' AW 23/24

Marlene Necklace
'World Wide Woman' AW 11/12

Marlene Parure, modelled by Masha Kirsanova,
'World Wide Woman' AW 11/12

Cherrie Long Earrings
Andreas Kronthaler for Vivienne Westwood 'The Tailor' AW 24/25

Embroidered Long Gloves
'War and Peace' SS 12

Rubina Earrings
Andreas Kronthaler for Vivienne Westwood 'Tintwistle' AW 23/24

Snail Brooch
'Summertime' SS 00

TINTWISTLE

Vivienne Westwood was born on 8 April 1941 in the village of Tintwistle. This picturesque settlement, nestled in the valleys of the Peak District, was to prove formative to Westwood's aesthetic. As she remarked of her idyllic childhood: 'Free to roam, I had a choice of three directions: the green hills of Derbyshire, the woods of Cheshire, the moors of Yorkshire.... My sister loved me to make fairy gardens on moss between the roots of trees. Climbing trees, jumping streams. I knew where every flower grew.'[16] Here was forged Westwood's love of nature. In delicate jewellery pieces, this takes the form of acorns and berries, snails and ladybirds, crows and wheat, flowers and foliage. Among the precious materials are marble, crystals, carved gemstones and lapis lazuli. In January 2023, Westwood was laid to rest in the churchyard of her beloved birthplace.

Bertille Necklace
Andreas Kronthaler for Vivienne Westwood 'La Nouvelle Eve' AW 22/23

Anglophilia Tiara
'Anglophilia' AW 02/03

Anglophilia Tiara, modelled by Tetyana Brazhnyk,
'Anglophilia' AW 02/03

Alphonsa Necklace
AW 17/18 Collection

Ladybird Earrings
Andreas Kronthaler for Vivienne Westwood 'Sous Le Ciel De Paris' SS 23

Myrtille Necklaces
Andreas Kronthaler for Vivienne Westwood 'La Nouvelle Eve' AW 22/23

Bertille Earrings
Andreas Kronthaler for Vivienne Westwood 'La Nouvelle Eve' AW 22/23

Lizzie Earrings
Andreas Kronthaler for Vivienne Westwood 'A&V' AW 17/18

Albine Earrings
Andreas Kronthaler for Vivienne Westwood 'Tintwistle' AW 23/24

Flower Skull Necklace
AW 08/09 Collection

Chloris Earrings
Andreas Kronthaler for Vivienne Westwood '43. Old Town' SS 24

Eva Choker, modelled by Eva Herzigová,
'Vive la Bagatelle' SS 97

Linda Choker
'Vive la Bagatelle' SS 97

Pastel Penis Necklace
'Chaos Point' AW 08/09

WONDERLAND

Vivienne Westwood's jewellery often explores notions of the fantastical and the fairy-tale, with exaggerated scale, unreal colours and bizarre juxtapositions of elements. Such pieces seem to have been pulled from imaginary stories; and, indeed, narrative was always an integral component of Westwood's design process – part of a rich and long-lasting heritage of storytelling through decorative arts. Here we can perceive a childlike sense of wonder and excitement, an innocence in naïve forms – but also a sophisticated game reminiscent of the Surrealists, displacing forks, cannabis leaves and other unexpected items onto the human body and reconstituting elements in novel materials such as stickers and textiles. A butterfly becomes a mask; rain clouds are transformed into earrings; a brass phallus is topped with a sugary pink bow. Whimsical and colourful, these humorous pieces – which sometimes verge on the grotesque – bring delight and joy.

Mimosa Pavé Earrings
Andreas Kronthaler for Vivienne Westwood 'Calibrate' SS 25

Azaela Necklace
Andreas Kronthaler for Vivienne Westwood 'Andreas' SS 18

Pastel Penis Pendant
'Chaos Point' AW 08/09

Pastel Penis Earrings
Andreas Kronthaler for Vivienne Westwood 'OK... It's Showtime' SS 19

Guinevere Necklace
Andreas Kronthaler for Vivienne Westwood 'Sexercise' AW 16/17

Ambra Mask
Andreas Kronthaler for Vivienne Westwood 'Sous Le Ciel De Paris' SS 23

Marie Jeanne Necklace
Andreas Kronthaler for Vivienne Westwood '7' AW 19/20

Marie Jeanne Sautoir and Earrings, modelled by Lara McGrath,
Andreas Kronthaler for Vivienne Westwood '7' AW 19/20

Lucianne Earrings
Andreas Kronthaler for Vivienne Westwood 'Sous Le Ciel De Paris' SS 23

Nymph Brooch
'Nymphs' SS 02

Nuggets Necklace
Andreas Kronthaler for Vivienne Westwood 'Tintwistle' AW 23/24

Rosa Necklace
Andreas Kronthaler for Vivienne Westwood 'Sous Le Ciel De Paris' SS 23

Giant Teddy Bear Necklace
Andreas Kronthaler for Vivienne Westwood 'OK... It's Showtime' SS 19

Lilian Alice Band
Andreas Kronthaler for Vivienne Westwood '12' SS 22

Therese Earring
Andreas Kronthaler for Vivienne Westwood 'Rock Me Amadeus' SS 20

Crystal Earrings
Andreas Kronthaler for Vivienne Westwood 'OK... It's Showtime' SS 19

DO IT YOURSELF

The idea of 'Do It Yourself' was in the bones of Vivienne Westwood, a self-taught designer. As a leader of the punk movement, she encouraged people to improvise their own clothes and accessories – a necklace of safety-pins, for instance, made at home. This was a deeply subversive proposition for any designer, shifting the power of creation from their own hands to others. The pieces here explore the idea of DIY through expressions of artisanship and elevation of commonplace objects, recycling and reusing ordinary items to extraordinary effect. Notions of bricolage – assemblages created from non-conventional materials, often discarded items and *objets trouvés* – are more commonly associated with modern art, but here they are applied to fashion. These ideas are especially radical in terms of jewellery – traditionally, a pure expression of affluence and status. Westwood's DIY ethos can be tied to her long-standing criticism of capitalism and over-consumption. As she noted: 'Reduce, reuse, recycle. Recycling is not enough to slow down climate change, but by reducing and reusing we can have real impact. One of the most important things I have probably ever said is: Buy less, choose well, make it last. It's all about quality, not quantity.'[17]

Simone Earrings
'Ultra Femininity' SS 05

Simone Earrings and Necklace, modelled by May Andersen,
'Ultra Femininity' SS 05

Key Necklace
'Street Theatre' SS 03

Leonida Neck Rings, Bangle, Choker and Earrings
Andreas Kronthaler for Vivienne Westwood 'The Tailor' AW 24/25

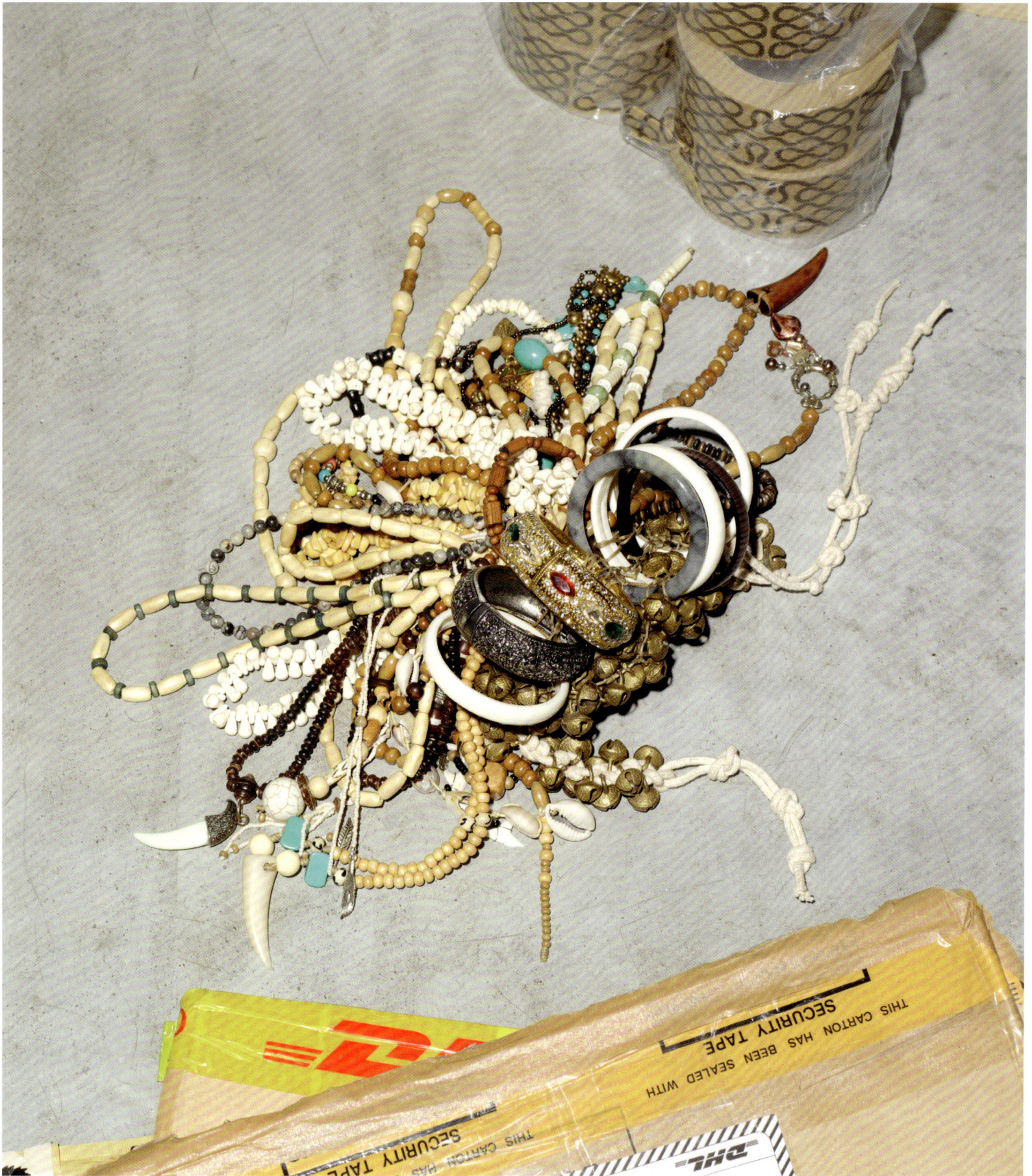

Persephone Wig
Andreas Kronthaler for Vivienne Westwood 'Rock Me Amadeus' SS 20

Persephone Wig
Andreas Kronthaler for Vivienne Westwood 'Rock Me Amadeus' SS 20

Detail of Key Necklace (see p. 114)
'Street Theatre' SS 03

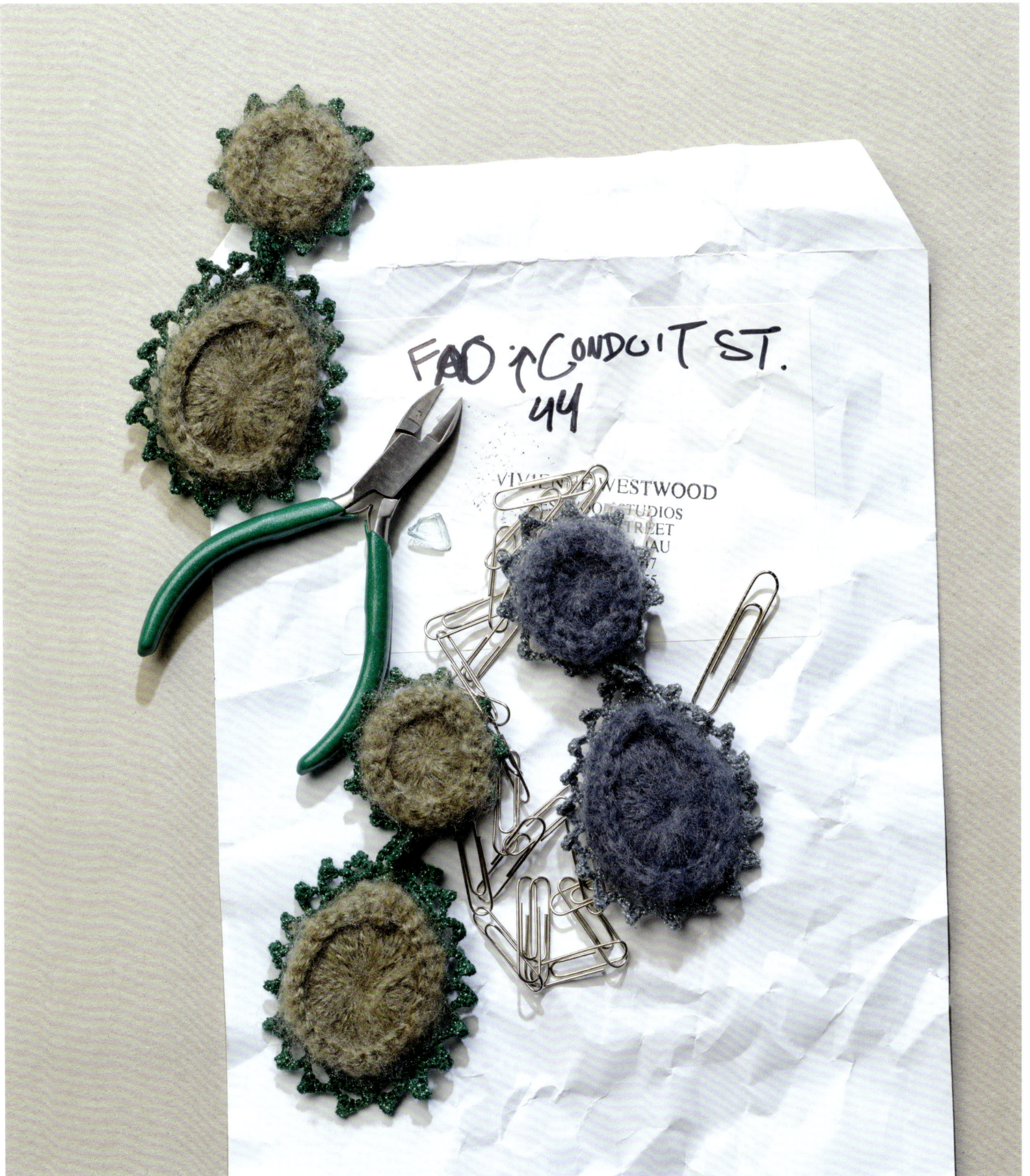

Crochet Earrings
'Winter' AW 00/01

Spoon Earrings
Andreas Kronthaler for Vivienne Westwood '7' AW 19/20

Giant Charm Belt

Andreas Kronthaler for Vivienne Westwood 'Vivienne' AW 18/19

Hortense Earrings

Andreas Kronthaler for Vivienne Westwood 'A&V' AW 17/18

Xaviere Necklace
'Gaia The Only One' SS 11

Benita Earrings

Andreas Kronthaler for Vivienne Westwood '12' SS 22

Lilian Heart Earrings
Andreas Kronthaler for Vivienne Westwood '12' SS 22

151

Benita Tiara

Andreas Kronthaler for Vivienne Westwood '12' SS 22

Renatta Necklace
'Mirror the World' SS 16

Muguette Necklace

Andreas Kronthaler for Vivienne Westwood 'Vivienne' AW 18/19

Anabella Pendant

'I am Expensiv' SS 07

Rosanna Earrings
'Europa' SS 17

Aloisa Earrings
'Europa' SS 17

Austrian Bangles
Andreas Kronthaler for Vivienne Westwood 'A&V' AW 17/18

Newyork Earrings
Andreas Kronthaler for Vivienne Westwood 'A&V' AW 17/18

MEMENTO MORI

In Vivienne Westwood's dark gems, we see a nod to the Tudor period. 'Cut, Slash & Pull' of Spring – Summer 1991 – the first collection where Andreas Kronthaler worked alongside Westwood through the entire creative process – was inspired in part by Tudor portraiture. Similarly, 'Five Centuries Ago' of Autumn – Winter 1997/98 took inspiration from 'Dynasties', an exhibition of Tudor and Jacobean portraits at London's Tate gallery. Slashed doublets, beribboned codpieces and provocative bodices, the striking realism of portraits by Hans Holbein the Younger, the golden age of Gloriana: these were rich sources for a new design vernacular. Here be dragons, penitence chains and studded chokers. Skulls and bones abound, but these are no literal historicist readings. An overarching character trait of Vivienne Westwood was a refusal to allow her intellect or her design aesthetic to be pigeonholed. Her creations are filled with contradictions and paradoxes, expressions of her deep belief in the philosopher Bertrand Russell's declaration that 'orthodoxy is the grave of intelligence'. Glittering skeletons and bejewelled funerary urns prove the point. As Andreas Kronthaler stated: 'There is a sacred value in making beauty.'[18] Here, the beauty takes the unexpected form of the charnel house.

Marcelita Choker
Andreas Kronthaler for Vivienne Westwood 'Tintwistle' AW 23/24

Armande Choker and Stud Choker
Andreas Kronthaler for Vivienne Westwood 'Calibrate' SS 25

Josephine Skull Necklace
'War and Peace' SS 12

Josephine Necklace
'War and Peace' SS 12

Josephine Tassel Earrings
'War and Peace' SS 12

Gilda Earrings
'Time to Act' AW 15/16

Elisabeth Choker
'Five Centuries Ago' AW 97/98

Elisabeth Necklace
'Five Centuries Ago' AW 97/98

Elisabeth Earrings
'Five Centuries Ago' AW 97/98

Elisabeth Necklace, modelled by Alek Wek,
'Five Centuries Ago' AW 97/98

Josephine Earrings
'War and Peace' SS 12

Zelda Necklace
Andreas Kronthaler for Vivienne Westwood 'Down to No. 10' SS 21

Memona Neck Ring
Andreas Kronthaler for Vivienne Westwood '43. Old Town' SS 24

Elisabeth Chain
'Five Centuries Ago' AW 97/98

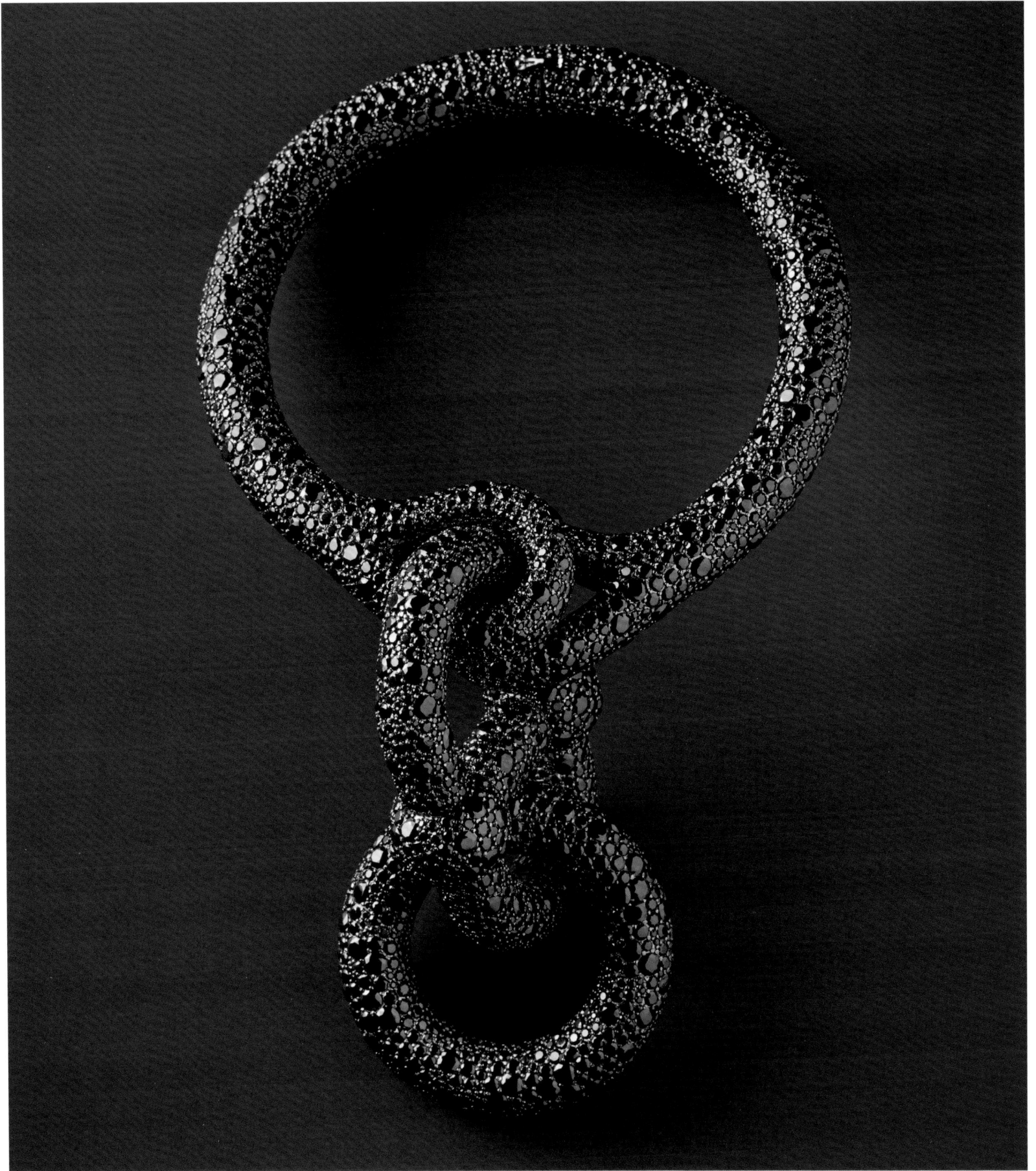

Zelda Pavé Necklace
Andreas Kronthaler for Vivienne Westwood 'Calibrate' SS 25

Embellished Corset

'London' AW 12/13

Flower Bone Brooches
'Anglophilia' AW 02/03

Bagatelle Long Earrings
'Vive la Bagatelle' SS 97

Bagatelle Sautoir
'Vive la Bagatelle' SS 97

Bagatelle Earrings
'Vive la Bagatelle' SS 97

Detail of Gilda Earrings (see p. 162)
'Time to Act' AW 15/16

Diamante Heart Pendant

SS 07 Collection

Andromeda Earrings
'Time to Act' AW 15/16

Elisabeth Medal
'Anglomania' AW 93/94

AR Pin Badge
'Active Resistance to Propaganda' SS 06

REGINA

Vivienne Westwood once stated, 'The only way to be original or find ideas is by looking at what people did in the past. You can't be original by just wanting to do something. Nothing comes from a vacuum. It is impossible to be creative unless you have a link with the past and tradition.'[19] Here, Westwood looked to the monarchy, to the Union Jack, to the unicorn and lion of the Sceptred Isle. Most famously, she looked to the regalia of royalty. The Westwood orb first featured as jewellery in the 'Harris Tweed' Autumn – Winter 1987/88 collection, which was partly inspired by the pre-teen princesses Elizabeth and Margaret in the 1930s. By adding a Saturn-inspired ring (a universal symbol of forward thinking and of exploration) to the traditional orb topped with a cross, Westwood instantly brought the past into the future. A Westwood tiara might sport devil's horns; regal earrings might swing with nude little satyrs; a pearl-encrusted brooch might carry a painted miniature portrait, but it is of Westwood devouring a phallic banana. Such pieces – resolute repudiations of conformity, and testaments to a constant reinvention of history as something new – are quintessentially Westwood.

Original Orb Pendant
'Time Machine' AW 88/89

Classic Orb Pendant, modelled by Kate Moss,
'Café Society' SS 94

Sarah Earrings
Andreas Kronthaler for Vivienne Westwood '12' SS 22

Fulco Earrings
Andreas Kronthaler for Vivienne Westwood '7' AW 19/20

Mistinguette Pendants
MAN SS 12

SEX Chokers
'Civilizade' SS 89

Ethel Brooch Set
Andreas Kronthaler for Vivienne Westwood 'La Nouvelle Eve' AW 22/23

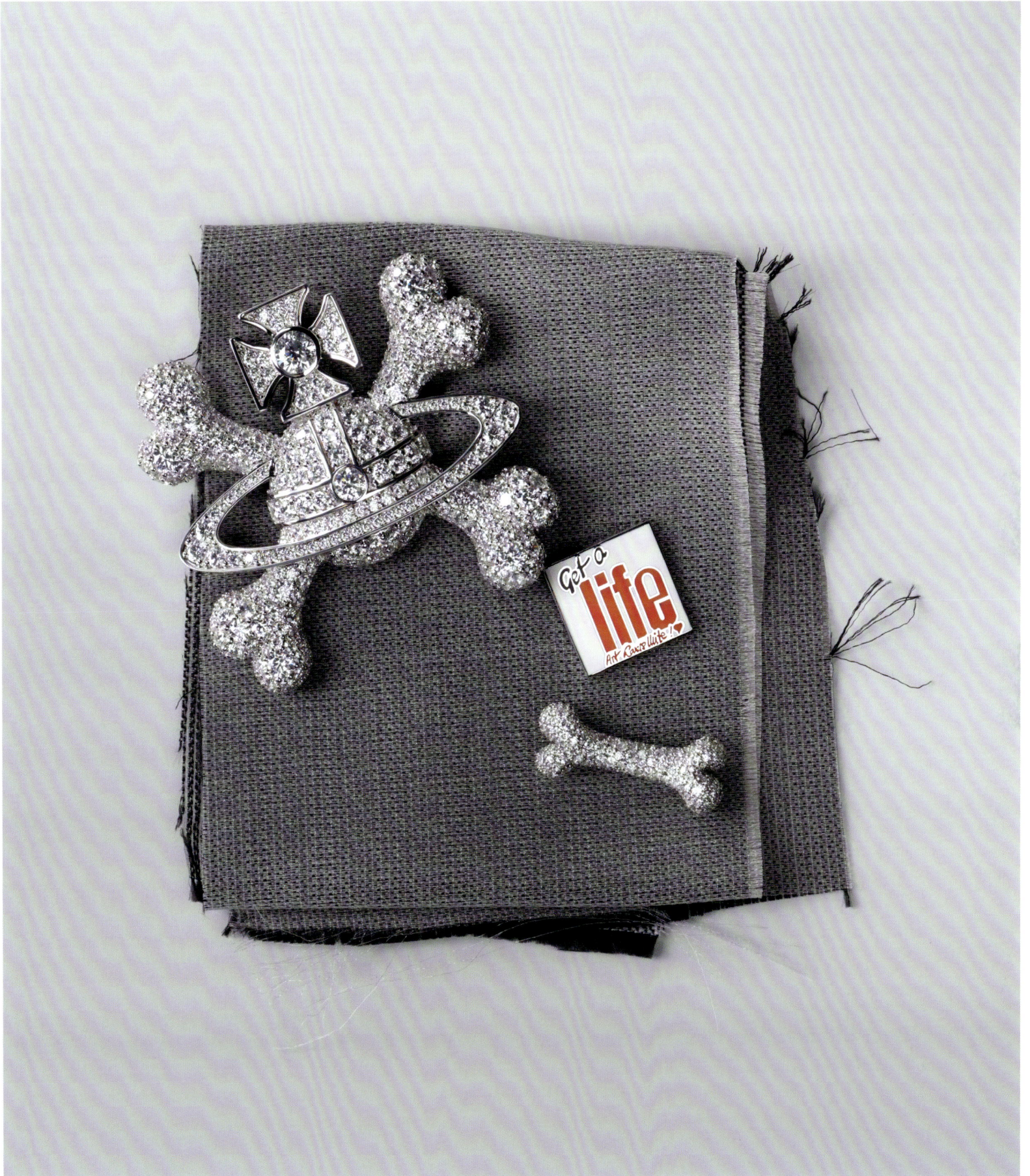

Crossbones Brooch
'Erotic Zones' SS 95

Get A Life Pin Badge
'End Ecocide' SS 15

Bagatelle Brooch
'Vive la Bagatelle' SS 97

Long Pearl Drop Necklace
'Five Centuries Ago' AW 97/98

Three Row Pearl Drop Necklace
'Portrait' AW 90/91

Horn Tiara
'Exhibition' AW 04/05

AR Pin Badge
'Climate Revolution' SS 13

THE ONLY
POSSIBLE EFFECT
ONE CAN HAVE
ON THE WORLD
IS THROUGH
UNPOPULAR IDEAS.
THEY ARE
THE ONLY
SUBVERSION.

VIVIENNE WESTWOOD [20]

PAGES 8–9 Andreas Kronthaler and Vivienne Westwood at the close of 'Rock Me Amadeus' SS 20

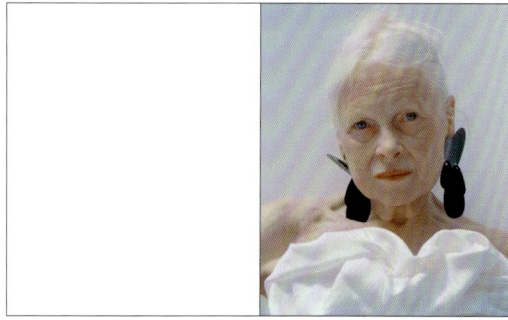

PAGE 13 *Magdalena Earrings*, Andreas Kronthaler for Vivienne Westwood 'Mayfair Lady' AW 21/22 campaign

PAGE 16 *Nose Ring*, modelled by Kate Moss, 'On Liberty' AW 94/95

PAGE 17 *Cream Cap*, modelled in 'Mirror the World' SS 16

PAGE 20 *Charms Necklaces Set*, modelled by Carla Bruni, 'Erotic Zones' SS 95

PAGE 21 *Giant Teddy Bear Necklace* (see p. 108), modelled by Idriss Marcus, Andreas Kronthaler for Vivienne Westwood 'OK… It's Showtime' SS 19

PAGE 26 *Anglomania Necklace*, Andreas Kronthaler for Vivienne Westwood 'Tintwistle' AW 23/24, oxidised brass

PAGE 28 *Pin Badges*, 'Climate Revolution' SS 13, steel, paper, plastic

PAGE 29 *Christa Brooch*, 'Europa' SS 17, gold and oxidised silver plated brass, oxidised brass, violet plated brass

PAGE 30 *Kate Safety Pin*, modelled by Kate Moss, 'Anglomania' AW 93/94

PAGE 31 *Kate Safety Pin*, 'Anglomania' AW 93/94, gold plated brass, glass pearl, crystal

PAGES 32–3 [LEFT] *S&M Earrings*, Andreas Kronthaler for Vivienne Westwood 'OK… It's Showtime' SS 19, gold and ruthenium plated brass; [CENTRE] *Shackle Earrings*, Andreas Kronthaler for Vivienne Westwood 'Vivienne' AW 18/19, gold and oxidised silver plated brass, resin; [RIGHT] *Malia Earrings*, Andreas Kronthaler for Vivienne Westwood 'Mayfair Lady' AW 21/22, oxidised brass, oxidised silver plated brass, glass

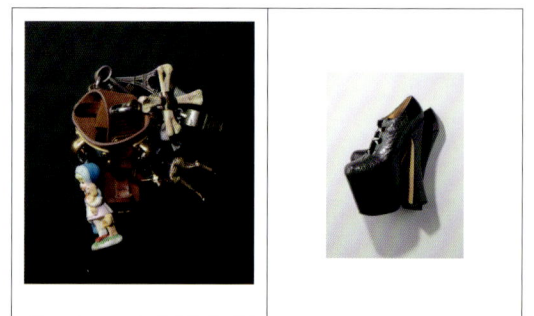

PAGE 34 *Gillian Choker*, Andreas Kronthaler for Vivienne Westwood 'The Tailor' AW 24/25, oxidised brass, oxidised silver and gold plated brass, leather, ceramic, chicken bones

PAGE 35 Super Elevated Ghillie Shoes, 'Anglomania' AW 93/94: 'Shoes must have very high heels and platforms to put women's beauty on a pedestal' – Vivienne Westwood

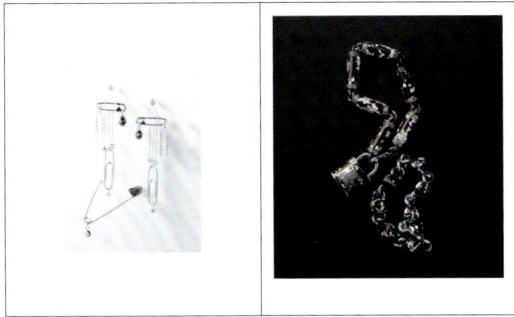

PAGE 36 *Hardcore Earrings*, 'Propaganda' AW 05/06, white gold, diamond, spinel

PAGE 37 [ABOVE] *Roman Necklace*, UNISEX SS 19, oxidised silver plated brass, synthetic gemstone; [BELOW] *Sigrid Choker*, Andreas Kronthaler for Vivienne Westwood 'Tintwistle' AW 23/24, oxidised silver plated brass, synthetic gemstone

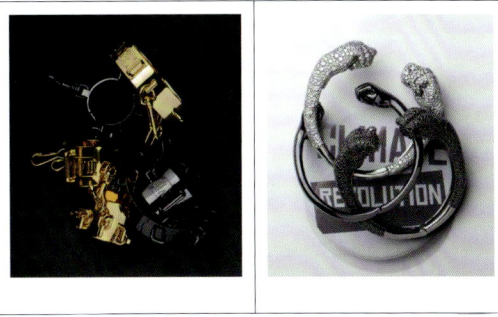

PAGE 38 [ABOVE LEFT & BELOW RIGHT] *S&M Cuffs*, Andreas Kronthaler for Vivienne Westwood 'OK... It's Showtime' SS 19, ruthenium plated brass; [BELOW LEFT] *S&M Cuffs*, SS 19, gold plated brass; [ABOVE RIGHT] *S&M Choker*, SS 19, gold plated brass; [BELOW RIGHT] *S&M Choker*, SS 19, ruthenium plated brass

PAGE 39 [ABOVE] *Cordelia Choker*, Andreas Kronthaler for Vivienne Westwood 'La Nouvelle Eve' AW 22/23, oxidised silver plated brass, cubic zirconia; [CENTRE] *Cordelia Choker*, AW 22/23, ruthenium plated brass; [BELOW] *Cordelia Choker*, AW 22/23, oxidised silver plated brass, cubic zirconia

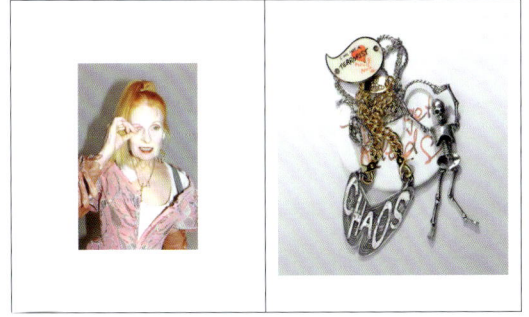

PAGE 40 *Skeleton Necklace and Earring*, 'On Liberty' AW 94/95

PAGE 41 [LEFT] *I Am Not a Terrorist Choker*, 'Ultra Femininity' SS 05, rhodium plated brass, paper, resin; [CENTRE] *Chaos Necklace*, 'World Wide Woman' AW 11/12, gold plated brass, oxidised brass; [RIGHT] *Giant Skeleton Necklace*, 'Climate Revolution' SS 13, oxidised silver plated brass

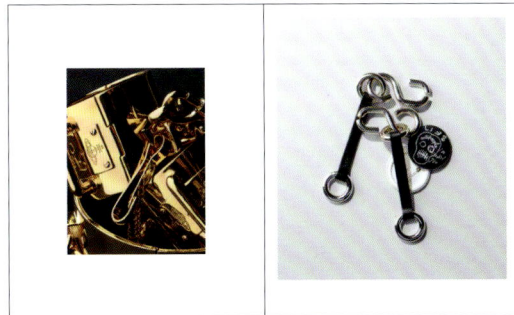

PAGE 42 [ABOVE] Detail of *S&M Cuffs* (see p. 38), Andreas Kronthaler for Vivienne Westwood 'OK... It's Showtime' SS 19, gold plated brass; [BELOW] Detail of *S&M Choker* (see p. 38), SS 19, gold plated brass

PAGE 43 *Curtain Hook Earrings*, Andreas Kronthaler for Vivienne Westwood 'OK... It's Showtime' SS 19, rhodium plated brass, leather

PAGE 44 *Broken Pearl Necklace*, 'Storm in a Teacup' AW 96/97, gold plated brass, glass pearl, crystal

PAGE 46 *Athena Necklace*, 'Erotic Zones' SS 95, gold plated brass, glass pearl, resin

PAGE 47 *Azaela Earrings*, Andreas Kronthaler for Vivienne Westwood 'Andreas' SS 18, oxidised silver plated brass, sticker

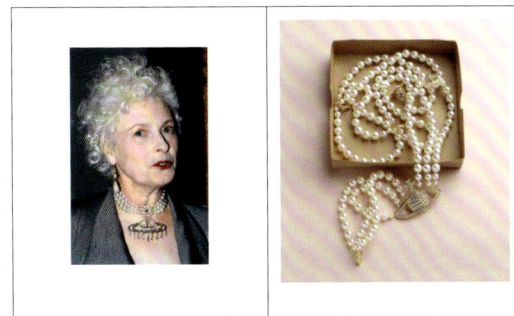

PAGE 48 *Gypsy Pearl Choker*, 'Erotic Zones' SS 95

PAGE 49 [ABOVE] *Three Row Pearl Drop Necklace*, 'Portrait' AW 90/91, gold plated brass, glass pearl, crystal; [BELOW] *Three Row Bas Relief Choker*, 'Salon' SS 92, gold plated brass, glass pearl, crystal

PAGE 50 [TOP] *Gabriella Neck Rings*, Andreas Kronthaler for Vivienne Westwood '43. Old Town' SS 24, pearl coating, brass; [BOTTOM] *Bagatelle Pearl Choker*, 'Vive la Bagatelle' SS 97, glass pearl, oxidised silver plated brass, cubic zirconia

PAGE 51 *Sidonie Earrings*, 'I am Expensiv' SS 07, oxidised silver plated brass, glass pearl, cubic zirconia

PAGE 52 *Gladys Earrings*, Andreas Kronthaler for Vivienne Westwood '43. Old Town' SS 24, oxidised silver plated brass, resin pearl

PAGE 53 *Loulia Earrings*, Andreas Kronthaler for Vivienne Westwood '12' SS 22, resin pearl, gold plated brass

PAGE 54 [LEFT] *Rosario Earring* (one of a pair), Andreas Kronthaler for Vivienne Westwood 'Vivienne' AW 18/19, freshwater pearl, gold and rhodium plated brass; [RIGHT] *Gina Earring* (one of a pair), Andreas Kronthaler for Vivienne Westwood '12' SS 22, gold plated brass, resin pearl, crystal

PAGE 55 *Athena Necklace* (see p. 46), modelled by Kate Moss, 'Erotic Zones' SS 95

PAGE 56 *Fulco Necklace*, Andreas Kronthaler for Vivienne Westwood '7' AW 19/20, pink gold plated brass, cubic zirconia, glass pearl

PAGE 57 *Venus Pearl Earrings*, Andreas Kronthaler for Vivienne Westwood 'Calibrate' SS 25, gold plated brass, resin pearl

PAGE 58 *Loulia Necklace*, Andreas Kronthaler for Vivienne Westwood '12' SS 22, resin pearl, gold plated brass

PAGE 59 *Nymph Earrings*, 'Nymphs' SS 02, oxidised silver plated brass, resin, cubic zirconia, glass pearl, mother of pearl

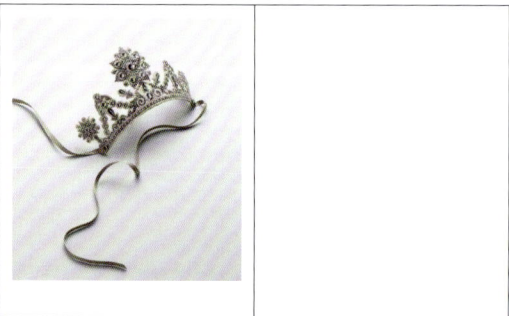

PAGE 60 *Papier Mâché Tiara*, 'Winter' AW 00/01, oxidised silver and ruthenium plated brass, papier mâché, textile

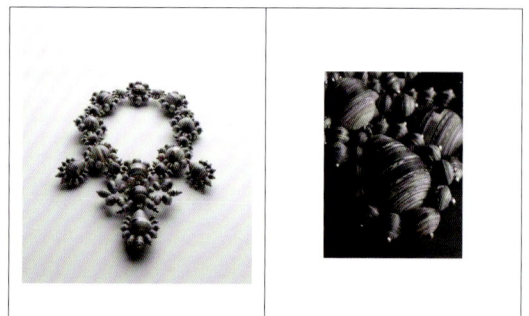

PAGE 62 *Papier Mâché Tiara and Earrings*, 'Winter' AW 00/01

PAGE 63 *Papier Mâché Earrings*, 'Winter' AW 00/01, oxidised silver and ruthenium plated brass, papier mâché

PAGES 64 & 65 *Josie Necklace*, Andreas Kronthaler for Vivienne Westwood 'Mayfair Lady' AW 21/22, oxidised silver plated brass, recycled paper

PAGE 66 *Gainsborough Necklace*, 'Climate Revolution' SS 13, oxidised silver plated brass

PAGE 67 *Gainsborough Coronet*, 'Climate Revolution' SS 13, oxidised silver plated brass, textile

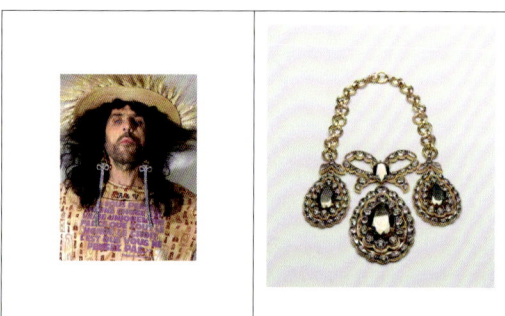

PAGE 68 *Justina Earrings*, modelled by Andreas Kronthaler, Andreas Kronthaler for Vivienne Westwood 'Down to No. 10' SS 21

PAGE 69 *Georgian Necklace*, AW 13/14 Collection, gold and oxidised silver plated brass, pyrite, crystal

PAGE 70 *Isaura Necklace*, Andreas Kronthaler for Vivienne Westwood 'Tintwistle' AW 23/24, gold plated brass, mirror, textile

PAGE 71 [ABOVE] *Isaura Tiara*, Andreas Kronthaler for Vivienne Westwood 'Tintwistle' AW 23/24, gold plated brass, mirror, textile; [BELOW] *Isaura Earrings*, AW 23/24, gold plated brass, mirror

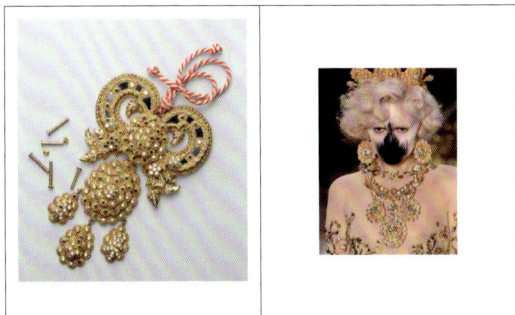

PAGE 72 *Marlene Necklace*, 'World Wide Woman' AW 11/12, papier mâché, mirror, gold plated brass, crystal, textile

PAGE 73 *Marlene Parure*, modelled by Masha Kirsanova, 'World Wide Woman' AW 11/12

PAGES 74 & 75 *Cherrie Long Earrings*, Andreas Kronthaler for Vivienne Westwood 'The Tailor' AW 24/25, gold plated brass, recycled can

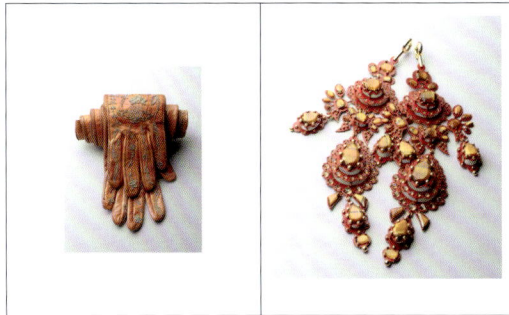

PAGE 76 Embroidered Long Gloves, 'War and Peace' SS 12: a key example of how embellishment is used on a garment, lending it a jewel-like quality

PAGE 77 *Rubina Earrings*, Andreas Kronthaler for Vivienne Westwood 'Tintwistle' AW 23/24, powder coating, gold plated brass, crystal, carnelian

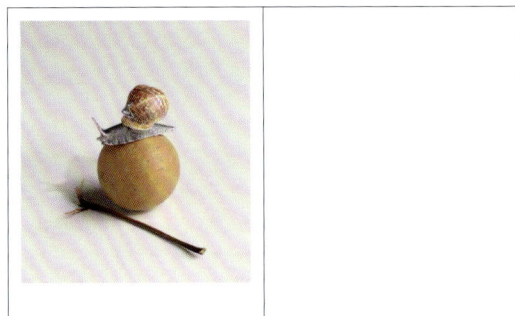

PAGE 78 *Snail Brooch*, 'Summertime' SS 00, oxidised silver plated brass, snail shell

PAGES 80 & 81 *Bertille Necklace*, Andreas Kronthaler for Vivienne Westwood 'La Nouvelle Eve' AW 22/23, oxidised silver and ruthenium plated brass, oxidised brass, crystal, various gemstones

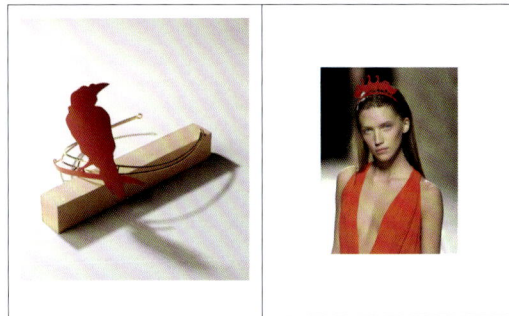

PAGE 82 *Anglophilia Tiara*, 'Anglophilia' AW 02/03, gold plated brass, powder coating

PAGE 83 *Anglophilia Tiara*, modelled by Tetyana Brazhnyk, 'Anglophilia' AW 02/03

PAGE 84 *Alphonsa Necklace*, AW 17/18 Collection, oxidised silver and gold plated brass, marble, cubic zirconia, glass

PAGE 85 *Ladybird Earrings*, Andreas Kronthaler for Vivienne Westwood 'Sous Le Ciel De Paris' SS 23, gold, oxidised silver, red, black and ruthenium plated brass, crystal

PAGE 86 *Myrtille Necklaces*, Andreas Kronthaler for Vivienne Westwood 'La Nouvelle Eve' AW 22/23, lapis lazuli, oxidised brass

PAGE 87 *Bertille Earrings*, Andreas Kronthaler for Vivienne Westwood 'La Nouvelle Eve' AW 22/23, black and gold plated brass, crystal, wood

PAGE 88 *Lizzie Earrings*, Andreas Kronthaler for Vivienne Westwood 'A&V' AW 17/18, gold plated brass, recycled biscuit tin

PAGE 89 *Albine Earrings*, Andreas Kronthaler for Vivienne Westwood 'Tintwistle' AW 23/24, mirror, gold plated brass

PAGE 90 *Flower Skull Necklace*, AW 08/09 Collection, rhodium plated brass, hand painted flowers, crystal

PAGE 91 *Chloris Earrings*, Andreas Kronthaler for Vivienne Westwood '43. Old Town' SS 24, gold plated brass, cubic zirconia

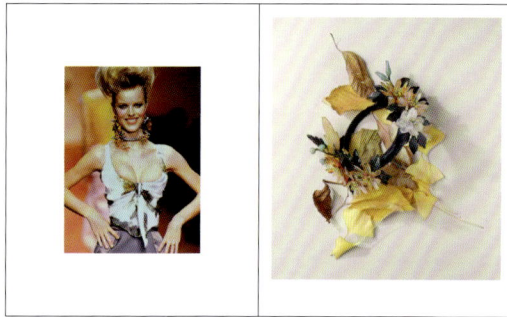

PAGE 92 *Eva Choker*, modelled by Eva Herzigová, 'Vive la Bagatelle' SS 97

PAGE 93 *Linda Choker*, 'Vive la Bagatelle' SS 97, gold plated brass, carved gemstone flowers, textile

PAGE 94 *Pastel Penis Necklace*, 'Chaos Point' AW 08/09, gold, pink gold and rhodium plated brass, crystal

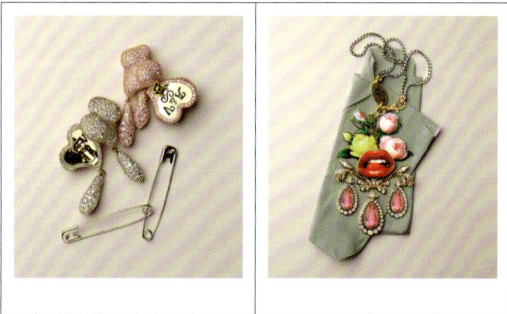

PAGE 96 [LEFT] *Mimosa Pavé Earrings*, Andreas Kronthaler for Vivienne Westwood 'Calibrate' SS 25, oxidised silver plated brass, cubic zirconia; [RIGHT] *Mimosa Pavé Earrings*, SS 25, pink gold plated brass, cubic zirconia

PAGE 97 *Azaela Necklace*, Andreas Kronthaler for Vivienne Westwood 'Andreas' SS 18, gold and oxidised silver plated brass, sticker

PAGE 98 *Pastel Penis Pendant*, 'Chaos Point' AW 08/09

PAGE 99 *Pastel Penis Earrings*, Andreas Kronthaler for Vivienne Westwood 'OK... It's Showtime' SS 19, gold and oxidised silver plated brass, crystal

PAGE 100 *Guinevere Necklace*, Andreas Kronthaler for Vivienne Westwood 'Sexercise' AW 16/17, oxidised silver plated brass, oxidised brass

PAGE 101 *Ambra Mask*, Andreas Kronthaler for Vivienne Westwood 'Sous Le Ciel De Paris' SS 23, oxidised brass, resin, textile

PAGE 102 *Marie Jeanne Necklace*, Andreas Kronthaler for Vivienne Westwood '7' AW 19/20, gold plated brass, oxidised brass, crystal, cubic zirconia

PAGE 103 *Marie Jeanne Sautoir and Earrings*, modelled by Lara McGrath, Andreas Kronthaler for Vivienne Westwood '7' AW 19/20

PAGE 104 *Lucianne Earrings*, Andreas Kronthaler for Vivienne Westwood 'Sous Le Ciel De Paris' SS 23, black and gold plated brass, crystal, onyx

PAGE 105 *Nymph Brooch*, 'Nymphs' SS 02, steel, gold and oxidised silver plated brass, crystal

PAGE 106 *Nuggets Necklace*, Andreas Kronthaler for Vivienne Westwood 'Tintwistle' AW 23/24, gold plated brass, glass

PAGE 107 *Rosa Necklace*, Andreas Kronthaler for Vivienne Westwood 'Sous Le Ciel De Paris' SS 23, red plated brass, crystal

PAGE 108 *Giant Teddy Bear Necklace*, Andreas Kronthaler for Vivienne Westwood 'OK... It's Showtime' SS 19, rhodium and gold plated brass, cubic zirconia

PAGE 109 *Lilian Alice Band*, Andreas Kronthaler for Vivienne Westwood '12' SS 22, ruthenium and red plated brass, crystal

PAGE 110 [LEFT] *Therese Earring* (one of a pair), Andreas Kronthaler for Vivienne Westwood 'Rock Me Amadeus' SS 20, scallop shell, aluminium, gold and violet plated brass; [RIGHT] *Crystal Earrings*, Andreas Kronthaler for Vivienne Westwood 'OK... It's Showtime' SS 19, crystal, aluminium, gold plated brass

PAGE 112 *Simone Earrings*, 'Ultra Femininity' SS 05, recycled can, oxidised brass, textile

PAGE 113 *Simone Earrings and Necklace*, modelled by May Andersen, 'Ultra Femininity' SS 05

PAGE 114 *Key Necklace*, 'Street Theatre' SS 03, ruthenium plated steel and brass

PAGE 115 *Leonida Neck Rings, Bangle, Choker and Earrings*, Andreas Kronthaler for Vivienne Westwood 'The Tailor' AW 24/25, recycled can, gold plated brass

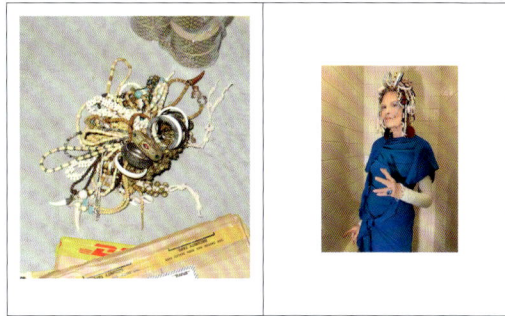

PAGE 116 *Persephone Wig*, Andreas Kronthaler for Vivienne Westwood 'Rock Me Amadeus' SS 20, recycled jewellery, glass, resin, wood, brass, textile

PAGE 117 *Persephone Wig*, Andreas Kronthaler for Vivienne Westwood 'Rock Me Amadeus' SS 20

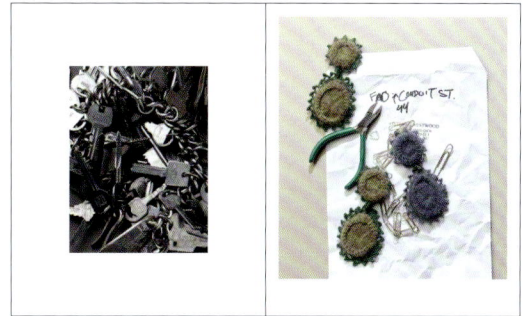

PAGE 118 Detail of *Key Necklace* (see p. 114), 'Street Theatre' SS 03, ruthenium plated steel and brass

PAGE 119 *Crochet Earrings*, 'Winter' AW 00/01, wool, gold plated brass

PAGE 120 *Spoon Earrings*, Andreas Kronthaler for Vivienne Westwood '7' AW 19/20, tin spoon, oxidised brass

PAGE 121 *Eurydice Earrings*, 'Ultra Femininity' SS 05, textile, crystal, ruthenium plated brass

PAGE 122 *Bird Watch Brooch*, 'Propaganda' AW 05/06, found objects, watch part, oxidised silver on brass

PAGE 123 *Garance Necklace*, 'Wild Beauty' AW 01/02, antique jewellery pieces, crystal, oxidised silver and pink gold plated brass

PAGE 124 *Zeta Pendant*, Andreas Kronthaler for Vivienne Westwood '9' AW 20/21

PAGE 125 *Bottle Necklace*, Andreas Kronthaler for Vivienne Westwood 'OK... It's Showtime' SS 19, broken glass bottles, textile, gold plated brass

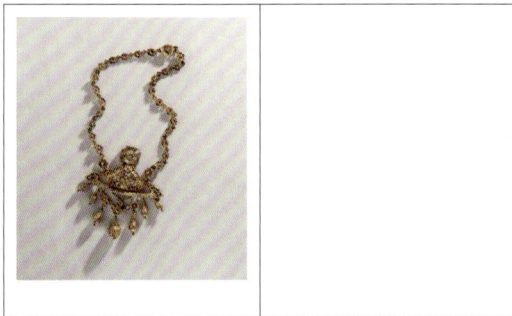

PAGE 126 *Delos Necklace*, SS 11 Collection, oxidised brass

PAGE 128 *Audrey Earrings*, modelled by Rosa Kirakosyan, Andreas Kronthaler for Vivienne Westwood '43. Old Town' SS 24

PAGE 129 *Audrey Earrings*, Andreas Kronthaler for Vivienne Westwood '43. Old Town' SS 24, resin, oxidised brass

PAGE 130 [OUTER] *Maddie Necklace*, 'Get a Life' SS 10, straw, gold plated brass; [INNER] *Liz Necklace*, SS 10, apple seeds

PAGE 131 *Maddie Earrings*, 'Get a Life' SS 10, straw, gold plated brass

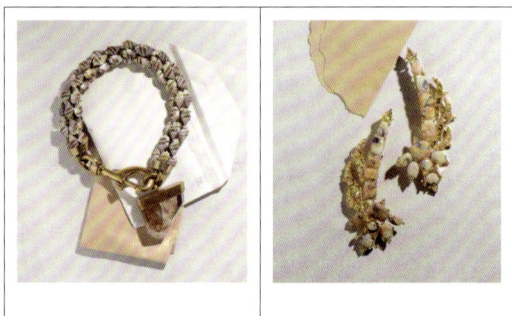

PAGE 132 *Philomena Necklace*, Andreas Kronthaler for Vivienne Westwood 'Calibrate' SS 25, oxi brass, cream shell, Himalayan quartz

PAGE 133 *Rosalyn Earrings*, Andreas Kronthaler for Vivienne Westwood '9' AW 20/21, crazy lace agate, cubic zirconia, gold plated brass

PAGE 134 *Greer Choker*, Andreas Kronthaler for Vivienne Westwood 'Calibrate' SS 25, straw, gold, rhodium and oxidised silver plated brass

PAGE 135 *Mariola Necklace*, Andreas Kronthaler for Vivienne Westwood 'Rock Me Amadeus' SS 20, various gemstones, crab claws, shell, glass, oxidised brass, gold, ruthenium and oxidised silver plated brass

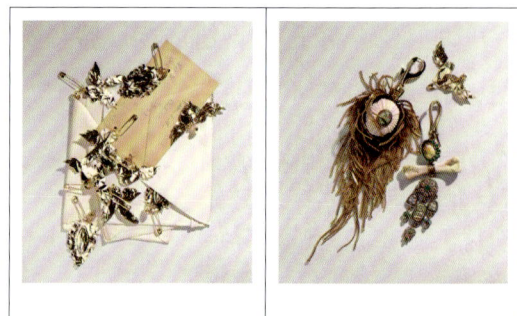

PAGE 136 *Delos Brooches*, 'Innocent' AW 06/07, gold plated brass

PAGE 137 [LEFT] *Rika Earring* (one of a pair), Andreas Kronthaler for Vivienne Westwood '12' SS 22, gold plated brass, sea urchin shell, ocean jasper; [ABOVE RIGHT] *Delos Brooch*, 'Innocent' AW 06/07, gold plated brass; [BELOW RIGHT] *Alexandra Earring* (one of a pair), Andreas Kronthaler for Vivienne Westwood 'Sexercise' AW 16/17, antique jewellery parts, chicken bone, oxidised brass

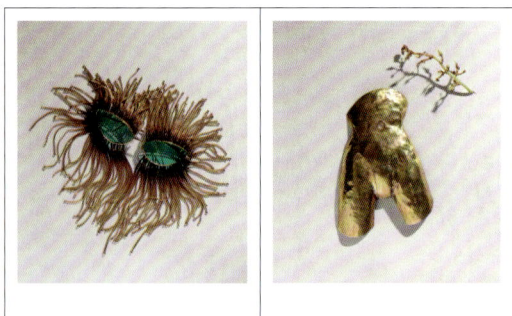

PAGE 138 *Rika Sunglasses*, Andreas Kronthaler for Vivienne Westwood '12' SS 22, gold plated brass, acrylic

PAGE 139 *Wilma Brooch*, 'Dressed to Scale' AW 98/99, oxidised brass

PAGE 140 *Neptune Earrings*, modelled by Sasha Krivosheya, Andreas Kronthaler for Vivienne Westwood 'Rock Me Amadeus' SS 20

PAGE 141 *Madeleine Necklace*, Andreas Kronthaler for Vivienne Westwood 'Rock Me Amadeus' SS 20, coins, crab claws, shell, glass, oxidised brass, gold, ruthenium and oxidised silver plated brass

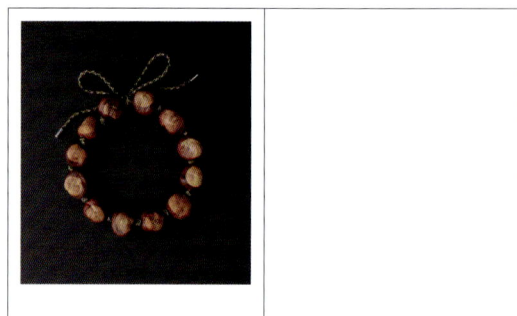

PAGE 142 *Conker Necklace*, Vivienne Westwood's Personal Collection, horse chestnut, silver plated brass, textile

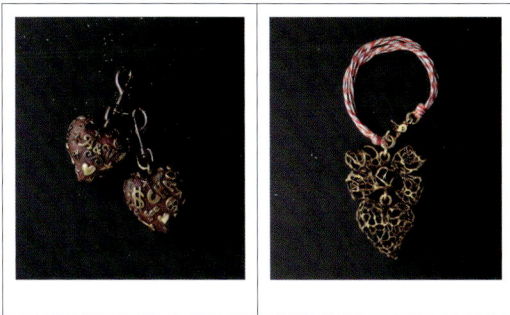

PAGE 144 *Florence Earrings*, Andreas Kronthaler for Vivienne Westwood 'OK... It's Showtime' SS 19, oxidised brass, wood

PAGE 145 *Pauletta Necklace*, 'Get a Life' SS 10, oxidised brass, gold plated brass, textile

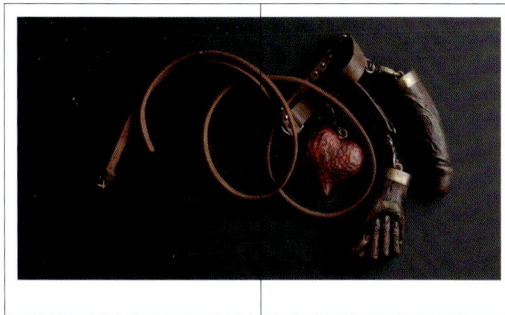

PAGES 146–7 *Giant Charm Belt*, Andreas Kronthaler for Vivienne Westwood 'Vivienne' AW 18/19, wood, oxidised brass, leather

PAGE 148 *Hortense Earrings*, Andreas Kronthaler for Vivienne Westwood 'A&V' AW 17/18, wood, oxidised brass

PAGE 149 *Xaviere Necklace*, 'Gaia The Only One' SS 11, coins, textile, oxidised silver plated brass, oxidised brass

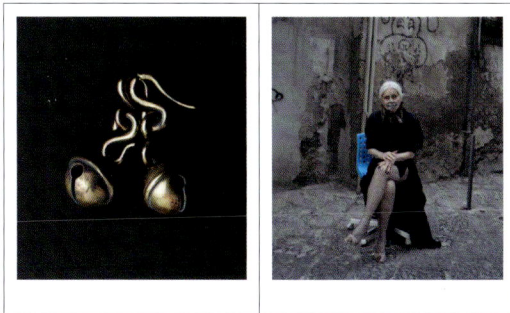

PAGE 150 *Benita Earrings*, Andreas Kronthaler for Vivienne Westwood '12' SS 22, resin bells, oxidised brass

PAGE 151 *Lilian Heart Earrings*, Andreas Kronthaler for Vivienne Westwood '12' SS 22

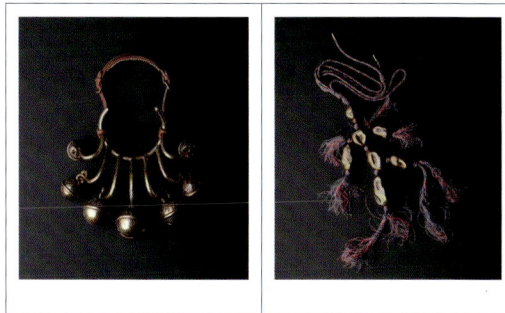

PAGE 152 *Benita Tiara*, Andreas Kronthaler for Vivienne Westwood '12' SS 22, resin bells, oxidised brass, leather, textile

PAGE 153 *Renatta Necklace*, 'Mirror the World' SS 16, resin, textiles, oxidised brass

PAGE 154 *Muguette Necklace*, Andreas Kronthaler for Vivienne Westwood 'Vivienne' AW 18/19, oxidised silver plated brass, oxidised brass, cubic zirconia, wood, Perspex

PAGE 155 *Anabella Pendant*, 'I am Expensiv' SS 07, oxidised brass, oxidised silver, oxidised copper

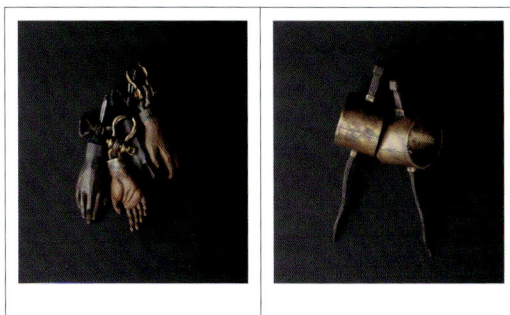

PAGE 156 [LEFT] *Rosanna Earrings*, 'Europa' SS 17, oxidised silver plated brass, wood; [RIGHT] *Aloisa Earrings*, SS 17, oxidised brass, wood

PAGE 157 *Austrian Bangles*, Andreas Kronthaler for Vivienne Westwood 'A&V' AW 17/18, oxidised brass, wood

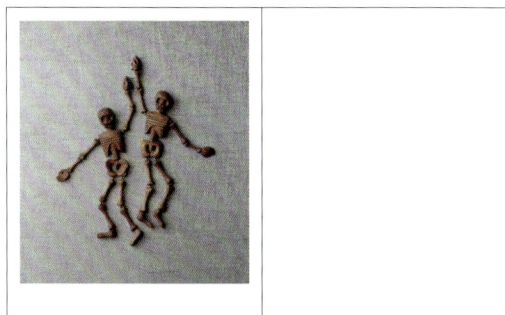

PAGE 158 *Newyork Earrings*, Andreas Kronthaler for Vivienne Westwood 'A&V' AW 17/18, wood, oxidised brass

PAGE 160 [LEFT] *Marcelita Choker*, Andreas Kronthaler for Vivienne Westwood 'Tintwistle' AW 23/24, gold plated brass, leather, gemstones; [CENTRE] *Armande Choker*, Andreas Kronthaler for Vivienne Westwood 'Calibrate' SS 25, oxidised brass, cubic zirconia; [RIGHT] *Armande Stud Choker*, SS 25, oxidised brass, cubic zirconia

PAGE 161 [LEFT] *Josephine Skull Necklace*, 'War and Peace' SS 12, resin, oxidised silver plated brass; [CENTRE] *Josephine Necklace*, SS 12, gold plated brass, oxidised silver plated brass, resin, textile, coins; [RIGHT] *Josephine Tassel Earrings*, SS 12, oxidised brass, resin, textile

PAGE 162 *Gilda Earrings*, 'Time to Act' AW 15/16, oxidised brass, oxidised silver plated brass, bumblebee jasper, cubic zirconia

PAGE 163 [ABOVE] *Elisabeth Choker*, 'Five Centuries Ago' AW 97/98, stones, freshwater pearl, gold plated brass, oxidised brass; [BELOW] *Elisabeth Necklace*, AW 97/98, stones, freshwater pearl, gold plated brass, oxidised brass

PAGE 164 *Elisabeth Earrings*, 'Five Centuries Ago' AW 97/98, oxidised brass, gold plated brass, gemstones, freshwater pearl

PAGE 165 *Elisabeth Necklace*, modelled by Alek Wek, 'Five Centuries Ago' AW 97/98

PAGE 166 *Josephine Earrings*, 'War and Peace' SS 12, oxidised brass, resin, ocean jasper

PAGE 167 *Zelda Necklace*, Andreas Kronthaler for Vivienne Westwood 'Down to No. 10' SS 21, ruthenium plated brass, oxidised brass, marble

PAGE 168 [TOP] *Memona Neck Ring*, Andreas Kronthaler for Vivienne Westwood '43. Old Town' SS 24, oxidised silver plated brass, cubic zirconia; [BOTTOM] *Elisabeth Chain*, 'Five Centuries Ago' AW 97/98, oxidised brass

PAGE 169 *Zelda Pavé Necklace*, Andreas Kronthaler for Vivienne Westwood 'Calibrate' SS 25, ruthenium plated brass, cubic zirconia

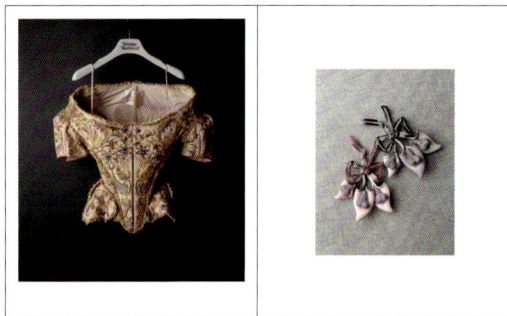

PAGE 170 Embellished Corset, 'London' AW 12/13: a key example of how embellishment is used on a garment, lending it a jewel-like quality

PAGE 171 *Flower Bone Brooches*, 'Anglophilia' AW 02/03, oxidised silver plated brass, brass, resin, crystal

PAGE 172 [ABOVE LEFT] *Bagatelle Long Earrings*, 'Vive la Bagatelle' SS 97, oxidised silver plated brass, cubic zirconia; [CENTRE] *Bagatelle Sautoir*, SS 97, oxidised silver plated brass, cubic zirconia; [BELOW RIGHT] *Bagatelle Earrings*, SS 97, oxidised silver plated brass, cubic zirconia

PAGE 173 Detail of *Gilda Earrings* (see p. 162), 'Time to Act' AW 15/16, oxidised brass, oxidised silver plated brass, bumblebee jasper, cubic zirconia

PAGE 174 *Diamante Heart Pendant*, SS 07 Collection

PAGE 175 *Andromeda Earrings*, 'Time to Act' AW 15/16, gold and oxidised silver plated brass, oxidised brass, cubic zirconia, bumblebee jasper

PAGE 176 [ABOVE] *Elisabeth Medal*, 'Anglomania' AW 93/94, gold and oxidised silver plated brass, textile; [BELOW] *AR Pin Badge*, 'Active Resistance to Propaganda' SS 06, gold plated brass, enamel

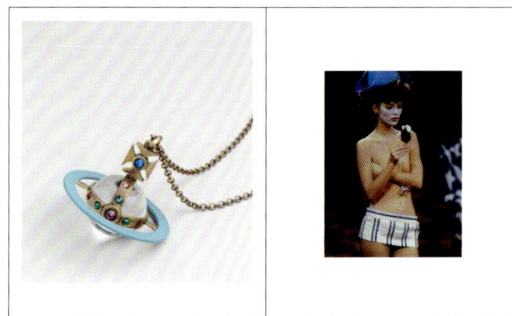

PAGE 178 *Original Orb Pendant*, 'Time Machine' AW 88/89, oxidised brass, Perspex ball, crystal

PAGE 179 *Classic Orb Pendant*, modelled by Kate Moss, 'Café Society' SS 94

PAGES 180–81 [LEFT] *Sarah Earrings*, Andreas Kronthaler for Vivienne Westwood '12' SS 22, gold and oxidised silver plated brass; [RIGHT] *Fulco Earrings*, Andreas Kronthaler for Vivienne Westwood '7' AW 19/20, gold and oxidised silver plated brass, cubic zirconia, glass pearl

PAGE 182 [LEFT] *Mistinguette Pendant*, MAN SS 12, oxidised silver plated brass, resin, crystal; [RIGHT] *Mistinguette Pendant*, SS 12, oxidised gold plated brass, resin, crystal

PAGE 183 *SEX Chokers*, 'Civilizade' SS 89, gold plated brass

PAGE 184 [ABOVE LEFT] *Ethel Penis Brooch*, Andreas Kronthaler for Vivienne Westwood 'La Nouvelle Eve' AW 22/23, oxidised silver and gold plated brass, glass, glass pearl, cubic zirconia, textile; [ABOVE RIGHT] *Ethel Andreas Brooch*, AW 22/23, oxidised silver plated brass, glass, glass pearl, cubic zirconia, textile, paper; [BELOW] *Ethel Vivienne Brooch*, AW 22/23, gold plated brass, glass, glass pearl, cubic zirconia, textile, paper

PAGE 185 [TOP] *Crossbones Brooch*, 'Erotic Zones' SS 95, rhodium plated brass, cubic zirconia; [CENTRE] *Get A Life Pin Badge*, 'End Ecocide' SS 15, rhodium plated brass, enamel; [BOTTOM] *Bagatelle Brooch*, 'Vive la Bagatelle' SS 97, rhodium plated brass, cubic zirconia

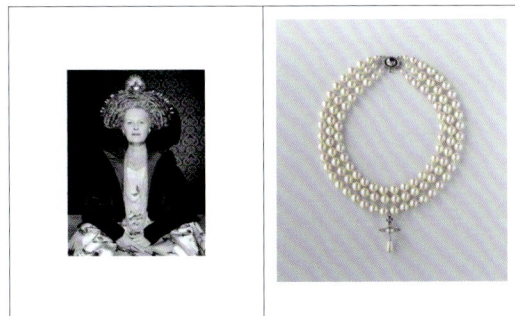

PAGE 186 *Long Pearl Drop Necklace*, 'Five Centuries Ago' AW 97/98

PAGE 187 *Three Row Pearl Drop Necklace*, 'Portrait' AW 90/91, glass pearl, rhodium plated brass, crystal

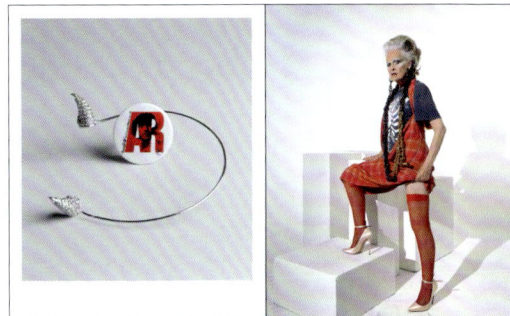

PAGE 188 [LEFT] *Horn Tiara*, 'Exhibition' AW 04/05, rhodium plated brass, crystal; [CENTRE] *AR Pin Badge*, 'Climate Revolution' SS 13, steel, paper, plastic

PAGE 202 *Zelda Long Necklace*, Andreas Kronthaler for Vivienne Westwood 'Down to No. 10' SS 21

PAGE 208 *Alexandra Earrings*, modelled by Tiffany Johnson, Andreas Kronthaler for Vivienne Westwood 'Sexercise' AW 16/17

PAGE 209 *Chloris Sunglasses*, modelled by Gendai Funato, Andreas Kronthaler for Vivienne Westwood '43. Old Town' SS 24

PAGE 210 *Amalia Earrings*, modelled by Amber Valletta, 'Vive la Cocotte' AW 95/96

PAGE 211 *Gypsy Earrings*, modelled by Eva Herzigová, 'Erotic Zones' SS 95

PAGES 212–13 Vivienne Westwood wearing *I Am Not a Terrorist Choker* (see p. 41), with Andreas Kronthaler wearing Vivienne Westwood pins, 2006

PAGES 214–15 Vivienne Westwood and Andreas Kronthaler at the close of 'War and Peace' SS 12

CREDITS

PICTURE CREDITS

NOTES

1. Author interview with Andreas Kronthaler, December 2023.

2. Ian Kelly and Vivienne Westwood, *Vivienne Westwood*, London: Picador, 2014, p. 73.

3. Ibid., p. 110.

4. Alexander Fury, with contributions by Vivienne Westwood and Andreas Kronthaler, *Vivienne Westwood Catwalk*, London: Thames & Hudson, 2021, p. 17.

5. Author interview with Andreas Kronthaler, December 2023.

6. Donald Watt (ed.), *Aldous Huxley: Critical Heritage*, London: Routledge, 1997, p. 51.

7. 'The Year of Punk', *The London Weekend Show*, presented by Janet Street Porter, London Weekend Television, 1978.

8. Ibid.

9. *Vivienne Westwood* (2014), p. 280.

10. Bertrand Russell, *Education and the Social Order*, London: Routledge, 2013, p. 16.

11. http://www.viviennewestwood.com (accessed 25 September 2024).

12. Kathleen Beckett, 'The Back Story on the TikTok Necklace', *The New York Times*, 6 July 2021, Section S, p. 6.

13. Jane Mulvagh, *Vivienne Westwood: An Unfashionable Life*, London: HarperCollins, 2003, p. 202.

14. See *Œuvres de La Bruyère*, Vol. 1, Paris: Frères Mame, 1808, p. XVIII.

15. Kathryn Flett, 'The Only Punk Left: Vivienne Westwood', *Harper's Bazaar*, 5 February 2013: www.harpersbazaar.com (accessed 4 February 2025).

16. *Vivienne Westwood Catwalk*, p. 16.

17. 'The World According to Vivienne Westwood', *The New York Times*, Turning Points Section, 5 December 2020, n.p.

18. Andreas Kronthaler for Vivienne Westwood Autumn – Winter 2019/20 ready-to-wear press release, cited in *Vivienne Westwood Catwalk*, p. 594.

19. Kristin Tice Studeman, 'Exclusive: Vivienne Westwood on the Art of Dressing, Costume, and More', US *Vogue*, 29 October 2014: www.vogue.com (accessed 4 February 2025).

20. Catherine McDermott, *Vivienne Westwood*, London: Carlton Books, 1999, p. 42.

ACKNOWLEDGMENTS

The publisher would like to thank Andreas Kronthaler, Carlo D'Amario, Alexander Fury, Laurent Rivaud, Philippe Lacombe, the contributing photographers and agencies, and members of the Vivienne Westwood team for their support in the making of this book: Giuseppe Aragoni, Eleanor Boyce, Phantanan Chantima, Dolce Cioffo, Christopher Di Pietro, Thiandanai Kanoungkid, Laura McCuaig, Katie Mitchell, Cinzia Nespoli, Chayanin Nusrimuang, Liz Sephton, Victoria Simon, Colette Thurlow and Ciro Tugnoli.

We would also like to acknowledge the groundbreaking work of Vivienne Westwood, whose empowering and subversive legacy continues to inspire generations of designers and activists alike.

ALEXANDER FURY is a fashion journalist, author, curator and critic. He is the Fashion Features Director At Large of *AnOther Magazine*, and the Men's Critic of the *Financial Times* newspaper. Previously he was made the first Chief Fashion Correspondent at *T: The New York Times Style Magazine*. He is the author of several books on fashion and luxury, including *Vivienne Westwood Catwalk*.

First published in the United Kingdom in 2025 by
Thames & Hudson Ltd, 6–24 Britannia Street, London WC1X 9JD

First published in the United States of America in 2025 by
Thames & Hudson Inc., 500 Fifth Avenue, New York, New York 10110

Designed by Stinsensqueeze

Photographs © Philippe Lacombe, unless otherwise stated

EU Authorised Representative: Interart S. A. R. L.
19 rue Charles Auray, 93500 Pantin, Paris, France
productsafety@thameshudson.co.uk
interart.fr

A CIP catalogue record for this book is available from the British Library

Library of Congress Control Number 2025936225

ISBN 978-0-500-02843-8
01

Printed and bound in China by C & C Offset Printing Co. Ltd

FSC
www.fsc.org
MIX
Paper | Supporting
responsible forestry
FSC® C008047

Be the first to know about our new releases,
exclusive content and author events by visiting
thamesandhudson.com
thamesandhudsonusa.com
thamesandhudson.com.au

Front cover: *Newyork Earrings, Andreas Kronthaler for Vivienne Westwood
'A&V' Autumn–Winter 2017/18* Photograph © Juergen Teller

Cover bellyband: *Elisabeth Medal from 'Anglomania' Autumn–Winter 1993/94
and AR Pin Badge from 'Active Resistance to Propaganda' Spring–Summer 2006*
Photograph © Philippe Lacombe

Endpapers: Montages by Vivienne Westwood

Front endpaper:
(from left to right) *Vivienne Westwood, 2017* Photograph © Juergen Teller;
Venus of Willendorf, Paleolithic Age, 29,500 years. Museum of Natural History, Vienna
Photograph Ganesh Krishnan/Alamy; *Vivienne Westwood, 1970s* Photograph courtesy
of the Vivienne Westwood Archive; *Athena Necklace, modelled by Kate Moss, 'Erotic Zones'
Spring–Summer 1995* Photograph Niall McInerney/Bloomsbury/Launchmetrics/Spotlight;
Jim French, Colt 69, Longhorns – Dance, 1969. Reproduced in the book The Colt Album,
published by John S. Barrington in 1973. Courtesy of the Estate of Jim French

Frontispiece:
Vivienne Westwood, 2017 Photograph © Juergen Teller

Back endpaper:
Andreas Kronthaler, 2013 Photograph © Maria Ziegelböck

(from left to right) *Rembrandt,* Self-Portrait in a Cap, *1630, etching.* The Norton
Simon Art Foundation, Pasadena (M.1977.32.010.G); *Vivienne Westwood in tiara,
Autumn–Winter 2000/01* Photograph © Jo Metson Scott; *Andreas Kronthaler,
2012 (detail)* Photograph © Xandra M. Linsin; *Andreas Kronthaler in Vivienne
Westwood menswear, Spring–Summer 2009* Photograph © Christian Anwander